Big Game on a Budget
by
Bob Gooch

Published by
Atlantic Publishing Co.
P.O. Box 67
Tabor City, NC 28463

ISBN 0-937866-58-X
Library of Congress Catalog Card No. 97-067976

To Michael, who doesn't hunt, but recognizes and supports the role hunting has played in the history of America and the role it continues to play in modern wild-life management.

Contents

ACKNOWLEDGMENTS

Who do you thank for help on a book devoted to hunting big game on a budget? A guide to economical, but successful hunting? Yes, the two are compatible.

In complete fairness I could go back over half a century or more of hunting and thank every partner with whom I have shared the fields, waters, and woods. They probably don't realize it, but all have contributed in one way or another to this effort. So to legions of hunting partners I say, "Thank you!"

Hopefully, many of them will read this book and recognize the author as a hunting partner from the past. Some I still hunt with. There's no way I can name them individually. Not all of them. To do so would fill this book with names, fine hunters all. Unfortunately, many of them, mentors of my early years, have gone on to their rewards on high. Among them are my late father who took me under his wing at an early age, and my mother who always took good care of the wild meat my somewhat tentative early hunting efforts brought to her kitchen.

Particularly helpful have been the professionals—the wildlife biologists, conservation officers, information people on the staffs of wildlife agencies throughout North America, public hunting area managers, refuge managers, and guides, outfitters, and others who serve the hunting public so well. Some have played a bigger role than others for no other reason than that I spent more time with them because of their particular expertise.

Forestry people of both national and state forests all over America have pointed the way to the good hunting areas, helped locate suitable campgrounds, and provided much invaluable information.

And last, but certainly not the least, is my wife Ginny. She has been a faithful traveling companion on treks all across America, even though she does not hunt. On long automobile trips we have split the time at the wheel, and she has often served as navigator using maps of various kinds to guide us into back country. Many times she has followed me into the field to shoot photos and make notes that I would probably not have had time for.

And when it comes to turning wild meat into tasty food for the table, she is unexcelled. Over the years she has learned to prepare with skill the likes of antelope, bear, boar, deer, elk, javelina, moose, and other game. Tasty and healthy fish and wild meat make up a major part of our diet—thanks to her skillful handling of it.

My daughters Pam and Pat have always been supportive even though they do not hunt. So have their husbands Jim and Michael. Jim hunts, Michael does not, but he strongly supports the right to hunt.

Have I overlooked anyone? Possibly, but that doesn't mean I am any less grateful for their help.

Thank you—each and all.

PREFACE

Nephew David, an Easterner like I am, wanted to go on a western big game hunt. He was new to the family, having recently married my niece. He suggested that Jim, my son-in-law, might like to go also. Knowing Jim's love for hunting, I was sure he was right. But how and still control costs? Both were young family men with mortgages and children to educate. After all, we live in Virginia, a good 36 hours by automobile from the nearest western hunting.

My mind began to spin. Good hunting. Not too costly, but a high chance of success. What were the possibilities? I could book a hunt with a number of western outfitters for a trip by pack train deep into the western wilderness, set up a hunt on a ranch and go for elk or mule deer, possibly arrange for a fly-in trip to some prime hunting territory, have someone drop us off by pack train or bush-plane in remote country, or we could pack camping gear and go it on our own. The last would be the least expensive. I doubted my young hunting partners would want to, or could, shell out the big bucks for the other possibilities.

Over the years I had used all of those approaches to some prime big game hunting, but I was thinking about David and Jim. Cost and time were serious considerations. They didn't like to be away from their young families very long.

How about a Wyoming antelope hunt? Plan it right and we were almost sure to bag our animals. Jim offered to drive his Jeep and tow my pop-up camper. We could drive straight through, stopping only for meals and to change drivers. We were facing a 36-hour drive, but by alternating at the driving we could all get in plenty of napping time. We would be in Wyoming the second day out in time to check into a motel for the night and awake rested and ready to set up camp and go hunting.

I called several ranchers in Wyoming and found one who would allow us to camp and hunt on his ranch at a modest fee of $200 each. He would also provide limited guide service , and we would have the ranch to ourselves for those three days. We could have eliminated the $200 fee by hunting public land and skipping the motel, but decided to allow ourselves those luxuries. It worked out fine. We all got our antelope before sunset of the first day. We then enjoyed some bonus prairie dog hunting while our meat was being processed and packed for the trip home.

We could probably have hunted mule deer using the same approach—and possibly even elk or other game.

But the point is we Americans can enjoy some of the finest big game hunting in the world and can do so on a budget. Our trip serves as a simple example of how those with limited financial resources can enjoy big game hunting on the North American continent. The chapters that follow will explain how.

Bob Gooch
Troy, Virginia

Big Game… on a budget

Chapter I

One Rifle Will Do it All

I was well along into a lifetime of hunting before I shot my first big game animal. As is true of so many modern big game hunters, that first out-sized critter was a white-tailed deer, a big one. It had a near perfect, well-balanced 8-point rack that hangs on the wall above my desk even as I beat out the first few pages of this long-planned book. I suspect the memory of that momentous event will remain with me as long as my memory functions.

We were rabbit hunting that long-ago winter day, my late father-in-law, his hunting partner Joe, and I, working a meadow between two small streams and moving slowly toward their confluence a short distance ahead when I spotted it. The big buck was standing on a small sandbar that formed the point at the confluence, peeking over the bank at our small party. For some reason our pack of little beagle hounds hadn't picked him up.

I was hunting with an Ithica Model 37 16-gauge repeating shotgun loaded with size 6 field loads, hardly the proper gun and load for a big deer. But that old buck stood there, holding his ground, and looking at us with only his neck, head, and those magnificent antlers showing above the creek bank. Not over 35 yards away at the most. I couldn't resist a try, maybe the chance of a lifetime.

Suddenly my shotgun was at my shoulder and I was actually aiming along the top of the barrel, something a shotgunner rarely does. Beyond the barrel those big antlers glistened in the weak January sun. Hesitantly, I hit the trigger. The deer dropped and disappeared behind the creek bank. Had I scored? I didn't believe I could have missed at that range.

I ran to the creek bank expecting to see a dead deer in the shallow creek. But instead I got a glimpse of my big buck racing away down the creek, his antlered head held high. I was sick. "Shouldn't have tried it," I moaned. "Just wounded that magnificent animal."

By then my hunting companions had joined me on the creek bank. "Look at those antlers," shouted my father-in-law. They had arrived just in time to see the deer bounding away—apparently unharmed.

"Let's take a look," someone suggested. "He might drop any minute."

And he did. We found the buck stone dead a couple of hundred yards down the creek, my first ever big game animal—and a trophy. My load of rabbit shot had caught him in the neck, but it took a few minutes for them to do the job.

That big deer made me a big game hunter. I was hooked, and determined to arm myself with a big game rifle before the next hunting season. But funds were short and I had all of the responsibilities of a young family man, a mortgage to pay off and two daughters to educate.

At the time the 30/30 caliber rifle was popular among deer hunters and less expensive than most more powerful rifles. I did a lot of shopping, visiting gun shops, and the hunting and fishing departments of the big stores. Finally a little Marlin 30/30 carbine caught my eye. I liked its pistol grip walnut stock and the short 20-inch barrel. It felt good in my hands, and it was well within my budget.

I added a box of ammunition and went home, set up a cardboard box with a hillside for a backstop and tried it out. The recoil was light and I was able to shoot a tight group. Later I took it to a gunsmith and had it fitted with peep sights, an improvement over the crude open sights.

When the deer season opened the next fall, I was out there early and within an hour I had a good head-on shot at a big buck. I held for its neck and hit the trigger. The deer spun at the crack of my little rifle and bounded away. I was too startled to even try a second shot. I immediately lost confidence in my little rifle, but my judgment was premature. I found the buck all but dead not 50 yards into the pine woods in which we had come face to face. A nice 9-pointer. A better animal than my first one.

I grew as a deer and big game hunter with that little rifle, falling in love with it in the process. For the next five years I got my deer early every season.

Finally, with a number of deer to my credit, I began to itch for bigger game. Eventually I was able to put a little money aside for an out-of-state trip and finally settled on a Newfoundland moose hunt. That was back in the 1960's and guide fees in the little province off the Canadian coast were amazingly low. Even the round trip fare from home in Virginia did not make a big dent in my bank account.

But I needed a more powerful rifle, something with more punch and better range than my little 30/30. I was talking to my Newfoundland guide about this later while on the hunt. I mentioned my 30/30 deer rifle. "That's what we hunt moose up here with all the time," he told me. He was talking about natives hunting for the larder. "We can get real close and shoot them in the neck," he added.

Maybe so, but I felt more comfortable with my 30/06 Remington 700 bolt action I had bought for the hunt. I'm not sure whether I loaded with 180- or 220-grain bullets for the trip. Either would have done the job. The moose is a big animal, but my new rifle handled the assignment. From a boulder high on a Newfoundland hill my guide and I spotted a good bull in a little valley below. "A good 200 yards," he said.

The moose was not aware of our presence so I took my time, removed my jacket and placed it on the boulder as a cushion for my rifle, rested the rifle on the folded jacket, and got the moose in my telescopic sights. My guide was monitoring the action through his binoculars. I took all the precautions (Marine Corps rifle range training), took a deep breath, released half of it, and settled the cross hairs of my scope behind the moose's shoulder. With my breathing under control, I squeezed the trigger ever so slowly. The report of the rifle almost surprised me, but I heard my guide exclaim "Good shot! But watch him. You might have to shoot again."

I didn't. The big animal reared up on his back legs once and then fell dead. "Let's go," said my guide. Elated, I pulled on my jacket, shouldered my rifle, and headed down to the meadow.

With a number of white-tailed deer and moose to my credit, I was ready for other big game. That came a few years later on the windy plains of Wyoming.

I talked a friend into joining me on a cheapie hunt for Wyoming antelope, an animal that has always fascinated me.

Most stories I read about antelope hunting talked of long, 300- to 400-yard shots in the flat plains country. "You need a rifle with a flat trajectory," was the usual advice. Feeling the need for such a rifle and doubting that my old 30/06 would do the trick, I went back into the rifle market. In the meantime, incidentally, that Remington 700 had replaced my 30/30 as a deer rifle. It had better range, more punch, and dropped the game in its tracks, whereas that was not always the case with the 30/30. I still own the little carbine, however, and have no thoughts of parting with it. It has brought me too many pleasant memories.

In my search for a flat shooting rifle I ended up with a Ruger 77 in .243 caliber. It's a fine little rifle that I use occasionally for deer. Its recoil is much lighter than that of the Remington 700 30/06 and its trajectory is flat.

Armed with my new Ruger, my friend and I drove through the night to Wyoming, arriving in time to set up camp for the following night. By 8 a.m. the next day I had my antelope—taken at less than 30 yards! Why. my old Marlin would have served me well in that instance. My friend took his antelope a few hours later at a much longer range. He was shooting a .270 bolt action, but I am not sure what brand it was. I still own that little Ruger .243 and use it occasionally for deer, but mostly for woodchucks.

I learned years later that my Remington 30/06 would have served me well on that antelope hunt—even for long-range shots. It came up when a friend planning an antelope hunt told me he was going to shoot his own 30/06, but load it with 125-grain bullets. That sent me scurrying to the ballistic tables where I found that actually there is little difference between the trajectory of the .243 and that of the 30/06 loaded with 125-grain bullets. One 125-grain soft-point 30/06 bullet sighted in 1.8 inches high at 100 yards will drop 3 inches at 250 yards and a little over 7.7 inches at 300. Compare that with one .243 bullet sighted in to hit 1.9 inches high at 100 yards which will drop 3.1 inches at 250 yards and 7.8 inches at 300 yards. The load of the .243 is incidentally l00 grains. For practical hunting purposes there is little to choose from between the two.

The 30/06 rifle with a bullet range of 125-grain to 220-grain will take any big game on the North American continent.

Review the ballistics of the ammunition of various manufacturers and you can come up with loads best suited for the particular kind of hunting you plan.

What this more or less told me is that I could have purchased a 30/06 back there when I went into the market for my 30/30 and enjoyed just as much success for all three species of big game—antelope, deer, and moose.

I don't regret buying the little 30/30 carbine or the .243 Ruger bolt action rifle. No regrets whatsoever. I enjoy buying and collecting guns, but I could have saved the costs of the two rifles. Besides I find occasional use for both of them.

With my Remington 30/06 bolt action I have bagged a great variety of North American big game, the likes of antelope, black bear, boar, caribou, elk, javelina, mule deer, musk-ox, and sheep. It has served me well from the swamps of Florida to the frozen Arctic, and from the deserts of Arizona and Mexico to the high country of Colorado and Idaho. While I am perfectly satisfied with my Remington bolt action there are like rifles of other leading firearms companies that are just as good. All will give you years of service.

I was in Alaska one summer on a camping and fishing trip and ran into an aging outfitter who had successfully guided numerous hunters for the big brown bears of the 49th state. "Will a 30/06 handle a brown bear?" I asked. "If you shoot 220-grain bullets it will," was his reply. Based on my own experience and that of the Alaskan brown bear guide, I feel safe in saying the 30/06 rifle will handle any big game in North America. It's the only rifle you need on the North American continent.

When I went from the Marlin carbine to the heavier bolt-action rifles, I mounted scopes on my hunting rifles. In my mind they add tremendously to the accuracy of the hunter. Most of my rifles are topped with variable telescopic sights, 3- to 9-power in most instances, but I'm not sure that choice of powers adds much. My scopes are all set on 4-power and I rarely have occasion to change them to a higher power. A fixed 4-power scope would probably serve me well. They are less expensive and probably a bit more durable.

Another choice I made was to stick as much as possible with bolt action rifles. The action is sturdy and reliable. I've never experienced a problem with my Remington 700 30/06, and I've hunted all over North America with it for over 30 years. All of my rifles except the Marlin 30/30 are bolt action, everything from my little .22 caliber rimfires to my reliable old 30/06. Regardless of whether I'm shooting squirrels or moose the action works the same—and it has

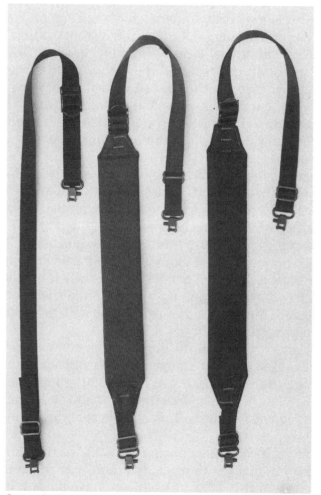

A good sling adds considerably to the utility of a big game rifle.

become second nature with me. I automatically work the bolt after a shot.

Another reason that influenced me in my choice of the 30/06 caliber is the availability of ammunition. It may not always be the exact load you are looking for, but it will work in most instances—even if you have to shoot a little javelina with 220-grain bullets.

The major thing the 30/06 rifle has going for it, however, is the wide choice of loads available. With ammunition ranging from 55-grain bullets to the heavy 220-grain loads you have a wide choice. That gives the caliber its versatility. Few, if any, other calibers offer that.

Most rifles come off the rack without slings. They require an additional layout of money, but they are worth every penny of the cost and they are a minor part of the total cost. Because of the recoil with the heavier loads, I removed the hard butt plate and replaced it with a shock-absorbing one. I still feel the kick of 220-grain bullets, but it is not punishing. Again, a minor change that will not cost you much.

A good rifle well cared for will last several lifetimes. In fact some never seem to wear out. Good care means primarily cleaning it fairly frequently— particularly during hunting seasons. I don't break my rifle down too far. Leave a more thorough cleaning to a reliable gunsmith. Wipe it lightly with a well-oiled cloth and give particular attention to the bore. A bore that is not cleaned fairly frequently will loose accuracy, and then only an accomplished gunsmith can give it the thorough cleaning needed to restore the accuracy of the rifle.

All rifles fresh from the gunshop have to be sighted in. This means setting up a target at 100 yards and firing and adjusting the sights until you get a tight group where you want it. Most hunters like to sight in their rifles a couple of inches high at 100 yards. This will put them right on target at 200.

You can save money buying a good used rifle. Just have a gunsmith check it thoroughly before you make a commitment to buy it. New or used, you have made a lifetime investment that you can pass on to the next generation.

Chapter II

Other Equipment

With a good rifle of your choice properly sighted-in, you can grab a handful of ammunition and go out and bag a black bear, wild boar, or some other critter that fits the description of big game. A few additional pieces of equipment, however, can help you enjoy your hunt more and add to your success.

But first let's take a look at ammunition.

As indicated in the last chapter, a wide choice of loads makes the 30/06 a highly versatile rifle, but which load you buy depends upon the kind of hunting and game you have in mind for a particular hunt. Let's take for example that 125-grain bullet sighted in at 100 yards. It will be 2.1 inches low at 200. But move up to 220 grains. Again sighted in at 100 yards, it's going to drop 6.8 inches at 200. In between there is a drop of only 2.3 inches at 200 for 150-grain bullets and 4.8 at 200 for a 180-grain bullet—both sighted in to hit right on at 100 yards. The drop will also vary somewhat depending upon what kind of bullet you shoot, for example, a soft-point or a bronze point. The difference between bullets is slight, however, as little as .1 inches— insignificant for hunting purposes. Let the weight of the bullet be your guide. Obviously the trajectory of a light bullet is going to be flatter than that of a very heavy one. But you might have to swap trajectory in favor of power for some game. You're going to need that 220-grain bullet for Kodiak bears, but they are usually taken at close ranges.

Study a ballistics table and note the variety of 30/06 bullets on the market—125 grain, 150-grain, 165-grain, 180-grain, and 220-grain. There are also a few variations in between these major weights.

While I used 220-grain bullets for my first moose, l80-grain would have done the job. I've used it successfully on most other big game, dropping to 125 for a flatter trajectory on an antelope hunt. Actually I shot that antelope at less than 50 yards! The trajectory I gained wasn't needed. I suspect the 220-grain is needed only for the big bears and possibly bison if you ever hunt them. Right now I'm shooting 150-grain soft-point bullets for white-tailed deer, but over the years I've taken deer with 125-, l60- and 180-grain bullets. I've stuck with l80-grain for black bear, boar, caribou, elk, and even for musk-ox. It's all a matter of measuring power against trajectory. Recoil is also a consideration. That of a 220-grain bullet will rattle your teeth, though I rarely notice it when firing at game. I suspect most experienced hunters will tell you this.

No experienced hunter feels comfortable without a hunting knife on his belt. In fact, he feels undressed. A good knife need not be an expensive investment, but you should go for quality. Like the rifle, a good knife is a lifetime investment. A good blade is the key. Look for one that will take a good edge and hold it for awhile. If it's too soft it will be easy to sharpen, but probably won't last you though the field dressing and butchering of a single deer. On the other hand, if it's too hard it will be difficult to sharpen. Determining this is not easy. Possibly the best advice is to buy from a reputable company that will back its product, and from a dealer who can give you advice. You can get good buys from the big discount houses, but not a lot of advice. There the best approach is to stick with name brands.

You might find what you want in the military surplus houses, though generally the military knives are a bit larger than most hunters like. To enter this market you need to know what you are looking for. If you find it, you will get a good knife and save a lot of money.

I have a little Buck sheath knife with a 6-inch blade that has served me well for a variety of big game. Often it has been no more than field dressing an animal, but over the years it has also been the primary butchering tool. Like most hunters, I've actually collected more knives than I need, but consider them prize possessions. I have a game warden friend, now retired, who worked good fall turkey country where hunters flushed turkeys, built a hasty blind, and then tried to call the scattered birds to the blind. "They would use their knives to gather material for the blind, lay the knife down, and forget about it," he said. Knowing this quirk of human nature, my warden friend made it a habit of searching around any abandoned blind he ran across and by doing so picked up a nice collection of knives. "Returned a few to their owners," he said, "but couldn't find most of them."

You will also need a sharpening tool to maintain a good edge on that knife. I still use a whetstone, but there are several more sophisticated sharpening tools on the market that do a better job. We are not talking about a major investment here.

A knife is an essential hunting tool if for no other use than field dressing an animal, but binoculars are not. They are handy, however, and every serious hunter should own a pair. They are particularly helpful to the still-hunter who studies the country for signs of game. They are also handy for studying an animal to see whether it is the trophy you

Binoculars are an important part of the big game hunter's accessories.

are looking for. Next to the rifle, binoculars are probably the most expensive item a hunter will invest in.

While on active duty with the Marine Corps soon after World War II, I picked up a fine pair of binoculars for a song at the post exchange. They were Japanese made. No brand name, but this was before the nation asserted itself as a leader in the optics field. Stay with name brands and you can save some money in the discount stores. The more powerful glasses are too bulky for most hunting. Something in the 10 x 50 range is a good choice. Here again you might well find what you want in the surplus military stores. Binoculars are a major item in the gear of artillery spotters—and they are usually good ones.

A rifle, knife, and binoculars are the more expensive items the big game hunter will have to acquire. Twenty feet of light rope is not costly!

Every hunter should own a compass. In fact they are required in some states or provinces. I was required to show a compass on a Nova Scotia hunt and one was required more recently on a deer hunt in the Great Dismal Swamp Wildlife Refuge in Virginia. Legal require-ments aside, no hunter should go into even semi-wil-

A compass is important regardless of how civilized your hunting grounds are.

derness without a compass. A compass is not costly. Here again you might find what you want in a military surplus store. Some fine compasses are made for military use, and they will serve the hunter as well.

Hunting knives and compasses can be carried on the hunter's belt and binoculars can be swung around his neck for ready use, but some items of need or comfort are best carried in a day or fanny pack. I used a day pack for years and later purchased a couple of fanny packs. Either will do the job, but depending upon what kind of hunting I'm doing and the game I'm hunting I may use either. I believe the day pack, which is carried on the shoulders, will hold more equipment, but the fanny pack has its advantages. For one thing the contents of a fanny pack are easier to remove.

It's mostly a matter of personal choice. Either pack will serve the hunter well. I suppose in some cases a hunter could actually use both! Strap the day pack on his shoulders and the fanny pack around his waist, but I've never tried it.

A pack is handy in many ways. For example, I dislike having either a camera or binoculars hanging around my neck. Carried in a pack, they are out of the way until you need them. You can pack your lunch and a small thermos jug in a pack and never notice them.

Portable tree stands are relatively new to hunting, but they have become very popular. White-tailed deer hunters probably use them more than any other kind of hunter, but bear hunters watching a bait often do so from a tree stand. So do wild boar hunters on occasion. Some hunters feel safer in a tree stand. Wild boar can't climb trees! There is a great variety of portable tree stands on the market and the elevated stands definitely give the hunter an advantage. He can see more and farther. A game animal might sneak by a hunter unnoticed if he is on the ground—but not as likely if he is way up there on a tree stand.

Poorly made tree stands can be dangerous, so when you go into the market make sure you understand what you are buying, and by all means make sure that a safety belt is included. The safety belt should be one you can attach to the trunk of the tree. So secured, you won't go far if the tree stand fails or if you lose your balance and fall from the stand. Since the advent of the portable tree stand, nasty falls have marred more than one hunter's season.

For most of the big game in America a tree stand is not appropriate. I doubt that many elk hunters use them. And they are certainly of no value to caribou hunters on the tundra, to polar bear hunters on an ice cap, or to antelope and mule deer hunters on the windswept plains of eastern Montana or Wyoming.

On unguided hunts, care of the game becomes the responsibility of the hunter. There is no guide along to take care of this for him. Care of the meat in camp should generally be limited to field dressing the animal and hanging it so air can circulate and cool the meat and keep it cool. Later, if he wants to pack it out or take it out by boat or canoe he might have to quarter the animal for ease in transporting. In the meantime while it is hanging in camp it's a good idea to protect the meat from insects. Game bags are needed for this. They are available in most hunting supply stores. They are white, made of cheesecloth, and porous enough to let in the air—but not the bugs. Depending upon the size of your hunting party and the number of animals you can take legally, you may need several of the bags. They are light, take up a minimum of room, and are easy to transport.

And about that nylon cord or rope. I like nylon because you can get plenty of strength in a small diameter. There are many uses for a length of strong cord. Twenty feet is a good length. Longer if you like. One of the first uses that comes to mind is pulling or lowering a rifle or bow up to a tree stand. Climbing up and down the ladder carrying a rifle or bow can be dangerous. It's much safer to pull it up and then lower it with that length of nylon line. In a pinch you can use it as a safety belt, running the line around the trunk of the tree and your waist and tying it securely. I can go on—hoisting an animal onto a game pole and tying it there or using the cord to pull an animal out of the woods to your vehicle. Many uses for that length of cord will come to mind when you get into a hunt.

And last but by no means the least important is a survival kit. Bare essentials include matches in a waterproof box, water purification tablets, a light poncho that can serve as a temporary shelter, a light ax, and a minimum of first aid supplies and snacks.

As a big game hunter gets into the pursuit of other game other items of equipment will come to mind, but this is a starter and certainly the most vital ones.

Chapter III

Shop for Clothing

There's an old saying that clothes make the man. I never agreed with that statement. It takes more than clothes to make a man. Much more. Nor does clothing make the hunter—though I have less of a problem with that statement.

The properly clothed hunter is a comfortable hunter, and a comfortable hunter is a more successful one. The hunter with cold and wet feet, numb fingers, and chills running down his back isn't going to be the alert hunter he needs to be for success. Comfort is a primary need the hunter seeks in his clothing. But almost as important in today's society, where just about every activity known to man is being questioned, is the need on the part of the hunter to make a good appearance. Appearance will also add to his sense of well being, but more importantly it will enhance the image of the hunter. A pair of hunters dressed like bums aren't going to impress anyone when they stop at a restaurant for lunch—except to send out the wrong message. "Hunters are bums." We need to correct that impression and dressing properly can help.

The hunter's clothing varies considerably depending upon what game he hunts, the kind of country he will hunt in, the likely weather he will have to deal with, and whether he will be hunting in a wilderness area or on the heels of civilization. These are some of the factors that will influence his choice of clothing. The hunter in Maine for moose, for example, will want different footwear than the elk hunter in the western Rockies.

When planning a trip, I like to mentally dress myself from the skin out. You add layers this way and stop when the needs to meet the hunting conditions are met.

Let's run through it.

I start with underwear. If the weather is going to be cold, I like the warmest kind I can find, but if it is going to be a hot weather hunt, the shorts and T-shirt I wear every day are fine. Regardless of the weather, I never pass up underwear. In hot weather it absorbs sweat, and if it's cold it traps the body heat and helps keep you warm on the coldest day.

Let's give first consideration to hunting in cold weather, the kind of weather most demanding of underwear. First I always go with long johns, and I prefer separate tops and bottoms instead of the traditional red long johns with the flap in back. Except in the warmest weather, I almost always wear the bottoms. They help protect my legs from briars, crawling insects, and other hazards. Tucked into my socks, they keep out the cold. I may forgo the tops if it's not too cold. I find that my outer clothing, which may consist of several layers, keeps my body warmer than does a single layer of trousers—which is usually the case. Blue jeans are a favorite of many hunters. They're tough, but not tough enough to turn back briars, and they don't provide a lot of warmth. You need that layer of underwear between them and your legs.

The choices of fabric in underwear is wide, cotton, polyester, silk, wool, and combinations of the various choices. Wool is warm for the colder climates and never a bad choice. It will shed water to a degree, but when it gets wet it gets heavy and the wetter the heavier. Silk is light, tough, and it, too, traps the body heat. Polyester is also popular and sold by many outdoor outfitting stores. Thermal is a popular name for winter underwear. "Let me go and get into my thermals." Quilted thermal underwear is a possibility, but it tends to be bulky. If the weather will not be too cold, October in the West for example, you can visit just about any store selling clothing for outdoor workers and find light cotton long johns that will serve you well, but for real cold weather I would go with wool or polyester.

I put on socks next and pull the tops up over the bottoms of my long johns.

A bowhunter dressed for changing weather conditions. He can peel off some clothing if necessary— or add on for cold weather as he is here.

Socks and shoes could well be the most important parts of the hunter's clothing. They protect the feet, feet called on to do a lot of walking and climbing—and seldom over easy terrain. Bruises, turned ankles, and frostbitten toes are often possibilities. You don't want to skimp on socks and shoes.

I first pull on silk sock liners. They are thin and help retain the body heat, though I'm not sure my feet hold much natural heat! I like wool socks because they absorb a lot of the shock of walking. They also absorb sweat, though sweating feet is rarely a problem except in warm weather. Combinations of wool and polyester are also good, so are wool and combinations of cotton, nylon, silk or other fabrics that wear better than wool, but retain the comfort and warmth of wool. It doesn't take much to put a hole in the heels of wool socks, comfortable though they are. I like socks that are just long enough to come a few inches above the tops of 10-inch boots. Either 10 or 12-inch lengths are fine, though I prefer the 10-inch lengths. Socks, more than any other item of clothing, should be changed daily on a hunt, so buy several pairs.

A shirt comes next, and here there is no better all-around choice than the age-old chamois cloth shirt. It may be a bit heavy for very warm weather and too light for very cold weather, but it will serve you well on most of the big game hunting you do. I like big pockets on my hunting shirts, two of them. They are handy for carrying a variety of small items such as a compass, game calls, truck keys, and the like.

For very cold weather there is no better choice in a shirt than wool flannel. I have a couple of shirts made of this fabric, but seldom is the weather cold enough for them. For warm weather light cotton is a good choice. It is soft and dries quickly should it get wet. Short sleeves are an option, though long ones are more appropriate for most hunting trips. Denim is a good in-between choice in shirts. It's tough, reasonably cool, and worn over thermal underwear in colder weather it provides a degree of warmth.

By all means buy shirts with long tails that cover the hips. This is a particularly good feature in cold weather for the warmth they provide. Short tails have a habit of working out of the trousers, an annoyance at the least.

Next come the trousers, and here we have all kinds or choices. I suspect that a survey of big game hunters would indicate that the majority of them wear blue jeans—or tough denim trousers. Certainly that is true on most western big game hunts. Jeans are fine, but make sure they have deep pockets. Pockets are the major objection I have

A properly dressed bowhunter with a good white-tailed deer. His face is painted with camouflage.

to blue jeans. The pockets are too shallow. Most jeans also fit too tightly. One solutions to that is to choose trousers that fit a bit loosely—maybe a larger size.

Fresh off of the rack, blue jeans tend to be hard—and stiff. They are noisy when worn in brushy country. Running them through the washing machine will help soften them, but plenty of wear is better. Well worn jeans are the best ones for hunting. For hunting in very cold weather jeans lined with thermal insulation are recommended.

For Canadian hunting I suspect you will find a lot more wool than denim in trousers. Wool is warm, of course, and very quiet. Rub it against the trunk of a tree and you won't hear it. That's important in still-hunting or stalking. But wool can get very heavy when wet, and that's its major drawback. Whipcord wool is harder and wears better and is the choice of many big game hunters in the northern United States and Canada. Combinations of wool and other material are a good all-around choice.

Hunting trousers, regardless of the material used, should be roomy, have deep pockets, and the belt loops should be large enough to accommodate a wide leather belt that will be called upon to carry a sheath knife and possibly other hunting items. And by all means make sure they are not so long that they drag at the heels. Hunting trousers should be much shorter than your street trousers. Cut them so that they drop to the ankles. Stag pants they are called. They drop over the tops of the boots, but not too far.

The belt is important. It need not be fancy, but it should have a strong buckle and be wide enough to hold a sheath knife comfortably. Narrow dress belts were never intended for hunting.

Pulling on trousers over boots or shoes is difficult so I pull on my trousers first and then turn to the boots or shoes. For years I've done just about all of my hunting, big game or otherwise, in the famous old L. L. Bean hunting boots. They are tough, durable, and will keep the feet dry and warm. They are fine for most eastern hunting, but in the desert country of the west I find that cactus and other sharp ground vegetation tends to pierce the rubber bottoms. I wore my old boots as late as yesterday for a black-powder deer hunt here in Virginia. I removed a pair of light hiking shoes and when I picked up the hunting boots I quickly noticed how much heavier they are. The hiking shoes are a combination of leather and Gore-Tex. I'm not about to desert my comfortable old Maine hunting boots, but for most western or high-country hunts I plan to go with the combination of leather and Gore-Tex. They cover my feet with tough leather that sharp cactus plants are not going to pierce. They are much lighter than my Maine hunting boots, and the cleated soles will provide better traction on some of those steep Western trails.

Now comes the outerwear, a coat or jacket. The age-old black and red mackinaw or parka is still a good choice, though there are other jackets that serve just as well—and possibly better in some cases. They are wool, but the more modern ones are lined with fleece or thermal for additional warmth. Such a jacket worn over a chamois cloth shirt and long johns is going to keep you warm in all but the coldest weather. It should have a large collar that can be turned up to protect the neck against cold, or better still, a hood that can be pulled over the head. Wool is good in a jacket, but Gore-Tex is also good. Both provide some protection against rain, but do not eliminate the need for a good rainsuit. Roomy pockets in which to warm the hands are a must. My old red and black jacket also has a lined game pocket in the back. I seldom use it for game, but it is handy for other items such as a camera or binoculars

A cap or hat, gloves, handkerchiefs, and a rainsuit will round out the big-game hunter's clothing. Throw in a pair of sunglasses if you like, though I seldom find use for them on big game hunting trips.

My preference in headwear is a stocking cap. It lacks a visor, of course, and rain can run down your face and neck, but this can be solved by pulling your hood over the cap— either the hood on your jacket or that on your rainsuit. Wear it under a hood and you have wonderful protection for your head. Caps with visors are fine if they also have ear flaps to protect the ears from the cold. Many western hunters prefer a brimmed hat. It sheds rain all around, but it offers limited warmth. One answer to that is to wear it over a stocking cap.

In very cold weather a balaclava, a combination of a stocking cap and face mask, will protect the face from the cold. Only the eyes are exposed.

The best hunting gloves I have come across are so-called "feel gloves" that have a thin covering for the trigger finger that allows you to handle your gun and shoot without removing them. They fit tightly around the wrist and can be shoved back beneath the cuffs of your jacket. I go through a pair every two years, but they are wonderful protection for the hands. In very cold weather a hand warmer that fits into the pocket of your jacket is welcome when after long hours the cold seeps through the fingers of your gloves. As in the case of socks, there are inner gloves of silk or other thin material that can be worn beneath your hunting gloves. They provide additional warmth.

A handkerchief serves many purposes on a hunting trip, but leave those white ones at home. Instead pack some red bandannas, large handkerchiefs that don't flash white when you use them. A careless hunter might mistake that white hanky for the white flag of a deer.

Don't forget your rainsuit. I stuff mine in the game pocket of my hunting jacket, but you can also put it in your day or fanny pack. Gore-Tex is fine though in a real downpour some water may seep through. It breathes, however, and lets in a little air.

Shop for clothing. Check discount houses, and visit the military surplus stores. My main objection to military clothing is that it tends to be too heavy for hunting purposes. But check it out. You might find just what you want at a true bargain.

An arctic hunt calls for special clothing. Clothing the average hunter never owns.

Chapter IV

Begin With Deer

I believe we can safely credit the comeback of the white-tailed deer for the growth of interest in big game hunting. Untold numbers of hunters who were perfectly happy with small game such as rabbits and squirrels suddenly became big game hunters with the mushrooming of the deer populations. Bigger game and more exciting game. And trophy hunting. A troubling side effect of this change in hunting interest is an alarming drop in small game hunting. This loss of interest in small game is a matter of concern among serious hunters and wildlife managers— but that's another story.

The dramatic comeback of the white-tailed deer is a wildlife management success story, an amazingly successful one, a feather in the hats of wildlife managers all over America. To a lesser degree the same can be said of the western deer, the mulie and the blacktail which is really a subspecies of the mule deer. The populations of the western deer, however, never got as dangerously low as did

those of the whitetail. In Virginia, for example, the state where whitetail hunting was born, there were less than 1,000 animals statewide a half century

The author with a Texas white-tailed deer.

ago. Today the populations are in the one million range—and still growing. In some areas deer have reached nuisance numbers and wildlife managers have liberalized bag limits significantly—and still the populations grow.

Today there is good white-tailed deer hunting in every state east of the Rocky Mountains, and the animals are being successfully introduced in many of the western states. Mule deer populations are on the increase from the eastern slopes of the Rocky Mountains west, and the blacktail deer are doing well up and down the West Coast.

We will talk here, however, primarily about the whitetail, the deer generally available to most hunters, particularly in the eastern half of the United States. The whitetail has learned to live on the heels of civilization. Suburbanites constantly complain about the pesky deer raiding their gardens. It's a problem wildlife managers constantly struggle with.

The late Jack O'Conner once said that the hunter who had good white-tailed hunting available need not feel sorry for himself even if he never hunted any other big game. The whitetail, particularly an old buck who has survived many hunting seasons, can be a real challenge. He's wise to hunters and their ways. I doubt if any other big game animal is more difficult to hunt.

There was once a rural store in my community, the epitome of the old country stores that sold just about anything a rural family needed. The owner also ran a farm and he was good about allowing neighbors to hunt. As was typical of country stores, his dwelling was close to the store, and just beyond his home was a small patch of hardwoods. A large field spread out behind his house and beyond that was a mixed pine and hardwood forest where deer hunters like to release their hounds. Hunting deer with hounds is popular in the community though I rarely hunt deer in that manner. A small stream forms just behind the storekeeper's house and follows a little valley through the field to the woods beyond.

A big old buck lived in those woods beyond the field and the storekeeper-farmer loved to watch him outwit the hunters. He would tell the story and chuckle.

The hunters would arrive and release their hounds in the edge of the woods beyond the field. The old buck would immediately recognize what was going on and sneak away. He would pick up the tiny stream and, using the scant concealment it offered, follow it to the woods beside my friend's house. "He would stay there all day," he chuckled, "and once the hunters and their hounds were gone he would go back to the big woods." That old buck lived to a ripe old age—and probably died a natural death.

Most hunters soon learn that the old bucks send the does ahead to test the possibility of danger. Experienced stand hunters tend to hold off temporarily when does appear, hoping a big buck might be following. Another trick that hound hunters deal with is the tendency of the bucks to let the does lead the hounds off on a wild chase while they sneak away, and circle back of the hunters.

That's the kind of critter the white-tailed trophy hunter is coping with. I doubt that any other big game in America can be more challenging. It's my contention that the successful white-tailed deer hunter will have no trouble adjusting to any other big game in America.

Learn and perfect your hunting techniques on white-tailed deer and then use those same techniques when you go after bigger game.

When I talk about deer hunting techniques, I'm thinking primarily of still-hunting, though some big game animals such as black bear and wild boar are taken from stands. They may be elevated or at ground level, but stands are more common on guided hunts than on self-guided ones. Hound hunting where hunters are placed on stands with the hope that the hounds will push a deer by them does not develop the skills that still-hunting does. Hunting deer with hounds is a rich tradition in some parts of the country and it can be exciting, but it simply will not prepare the hunter for most other big game.

Because most hunters find deer the most accessible of the big game species, they usually begin their big-game hunting careers there. Fortunately there is no better training. Hunters learn the pleasures and rewards of hunting the white-tailed deer and eventually develop a yen for

Big Game... on a budget

Mule deer are found throughout the West and can be taken on private ranches or public land by hunters camping nearby or headquartered in a motel.

other big game. So begins a never-ending quest for what might appear to be a never-ending array of big game animals. The North American continent is ripe in big-game variety. The hunter on a time and money budget, as most of us are, can spend a lifetime in the pursuit of American big game. Eventually there is Africa and other foreign hunting which becomes little more than a dream for many of us. That's good in that there is always still another big-game animal on the horizon or just over the hill. Always another goal to seek. It can keep a hunter happy and healthy for a long life.

Of the various methods used to hunt deer, I feel the best training is still-hunting. It can be used for a great variety of big game, particularly for a member of the large deer family—elk, moose, mule deer, and blacktail deer among others. The successful still-hunter first knows his quarry, its habits and its senses of protection. He knows, for example, that deer tend to feed at night when the moon is full and the nights are bright. They bed down at dawn and may not begin feeding again until noon.

The still-hunter also recognizes the deer's three senses of protection: smell, hearing, and vision in that order. To combat smell the hunter knows he has to work into the wind if possible or at least crosswise to it. Never with the wind at his back. A whiff of his scent hits a deer and he's gone long before he sees his quarry.

He also knows that the deer's sense of hearing is excellent. Sure there are all kinds of sounds in the woods, but the deer recognizes them, is attuned to them, but it will immediately detect a strange sound. A hunter coughs, for example, or sneezes. He steps on a piece of dead wood and it snaps. Or he brushes against a piece of vegetation creating a sound strange to the woods—and to the deer. He combats this strong sense by wearing clothing that does not rustle, soft finished clothing such as wool or well-washed cotton. Rubbed against a twig or small sapling, this kind of clothing is noiseless. He also learns how to move as quietly and inconspicuously as possible, picking his route carefully and watching where he places his feet. Actually he moves only short distances at a time concentrating on the moving and doing his looking and listening when he pauses. A good still-hunter does not cover a great amount of distance in a few hours, but he works hard on what terrain he does hunt.

The senses of smell and hearing are strong in most big game animals, their first line of defense, but their ability to see varies among species. The deer's vision does not permit it to distinguish between colors, so hunter orange does not present a problem—if the hunter is not moving. A deer can detect movement regardless of the color of the object that is moving. For that reason a deer hunter tries to use concealment as he moves. It may take the form of a ditch, vegetation, streambed, the trunk of a big tree and so on. Once he spots game, the still-hunter concentrates on getting in position for a good shot. He may be already within range, but wants to move to a better position, possibly one that offers a rest for his rifle. Keeping the animal in view, he moves only when its head is down—usually feeding. If the animal suddenly lifts its head indicating it has been alerted, the hunter freezes and remains frozen until the deer resumes its feeding.

Almost as valuable to a still-hunter as his rifle is a pair of binoculars. Binoculars will reveal so much more than the naked eye. Some hunters use the scopes on their rifles for studying the country they are hunting, but a scope is awkward and a poor substitute. Viewing his hunting territory through glasses enables the hunter to pick up small things that he might never see with his naked eye. The flap of an ear, the swish of a tail, movement of a foot, the sun glinting off of a set of antlers, or even a shiny dark eye that stands out from the excellent natural camouflage the animal may be taking advantage of. Binoculars are also valuable for studying a possible trophy animal, to count the points, and to determine if that's the trophy they want. If not, they pass up a shot and hope for a better one.

The good thing about deer is that you seldom have to travel far to hunt them, certainly not out of state in most cases. Nor even out of your county or township in others.

Probably in most parts of any state the very best deer hunting is on private land, particularly in the case of whitetails. Getting permission to hunt those lands can be a problem. Some hunters form clubs and lease private land. It's the surest way of having some good hunting territory close by. Sometimes simply asking farmers for permission can be rewarding. Or maybe you have family members or friends who own land. Even small tracts might hold deer. The whitetail doesn't need much—some woodlands for acorns, some nearby grasslands to graze, and some thickets or swamps to hide in. A 10-acre plot with the right combination of cover and food can provide some good hunting, hunting that others may never think about.

In the western part of America there are millions of acres of public land in most states. It might be state-owned public hunting land, but more likely national forests or lands controlled by the Bureau of Land Management. There is so much public land in the West that a hunter who doesn't mind doing a little hiking can get away from the crowd. National forests, state forests, and public hunting lands are also reasonably abundant in the eastern part of America. Some states have millions of acres of public lands while there is precious little in others. But there is some public land open to the public in just about every state.

For those who have yet to down their first big game animal, the white-tailed deer is the way to begin. And for those who are already experienced deer hunters, there is other game out there to try those well-honed techniques on.

Not since the days of Teddy Roosevelt has big game hunting been as good and as widespread as it is in America today. Polish your skills on the whitetail and then sample the other possibilities.

Chapter V

Other Accessible Big Game Hunting

Without a doubt, between them mule and white-tailed deer offer the most accessible big game hunting in America—and they are the hardest hunted. Of the two, the whitetail is the most available to the majority of hunters because its native range is extensive and it has been successfully introduced far beyond that original range, particularly in the western United States.

Though not considered game animals in many states coyotes are found just about all over the United States and offer some exciting and interesting hunting.

Beyond the deer, quick access to big game hunting drops off quickly with the possible exception of the wild turkey. Many wildlife managers, however, consider the wild turkey a gamebird instead of big game. It's both. It is a magnificent gamebird, but it is also considered big game by other wildlife managers and by most hunters. Here it will be considered big game because it is hunted much as big game is hunted, the bag limits are

Some states consider the wild turkey a game bird, but others consider it big game. It is classified as big game in this book. Every state in the United States and a few Canadian provinces offer turkey hunting.

low as is the case with big game, and it's a trophy bird. The big game license in Virginia, my home state, has tags for bear, deer, and turkeys. An old gobbler with a long beard and spurs on its legs is a true trophy. Big gobblers are entered in many big game contests. In many states the season limit is still one bird. Rarely do gamebirds get that kind of protection.

The comeback of the wild turkey has been equally as dramatic as that of the white-tailed deer. There have always been a few wild turkeys around. Virginia, for example, where Captain John Smith and his hardy little band lived through their first harsh winter on Jamestown Island, has never been without a wild turkey hunting season. Those hardy men lived mostly on deer, turkeys, and other game. In Massachusetts turkeys were all but extinct over a century ago, but are now back in huntable numbers. In some western states such as arid Nevada, there were never any turkeys until the modern miracle of good wildlife management introduced the birds. Today every state except Alaska, which is simply too cold for the birds, has open seasons on wild turkeys.

There are spring seasons in all states where gobblers only are legal. An exception is Hawaii where the seasons are all but indistinguishable. A number of states offer fall and winter hunting in addition to spring hunting. In fact, approximately half of the states have fall and winter turkey seasons. Many of them are the older turkey hunting states where fall hunting has a rich tradition. Typically when turkeys are introduced or reintroduced to a new state, hunting begins with a spring season. Gobblers only are legal then and removing some of the old toms does not hurt the developing populations. Some good turkey hunting states never get beyond spring seasons.

The wild turkey can easily become the next step for the hunter moving from deer to other big game. Not that the turkey is easy to hunt, but today there is turkey hunting in every state, and usually even better turkey hunting isn't far away if that at home is limited. Turkeys can be a real challenge. Many big game hunters who have a number of species to their credit say the wary turkey, particularly an old gobbler, is the most difficult of all. Either fall or spring, the developing big game hunter can learn a lot on turkeys—and very inexpensively.

The novice turkey hunter is probably best off breaking in during the spring season. There is a season in every state except Alaska, and getting into spring hunting is a little less complicated than fall hunting where the use of good turkey dogs is a popular hunting method.

The novice spring hunter should buy a video or two on turkey calling or take in a turkey hunting school where calling is part of the instruction. Once calling is mastered she or he is ready for the turkey woods.

Calling will also work in the fall and winter, but it's not as effective as in the spring. A gobbler may respond, but not always. A spring gobbler is more likely to do so. One approach to fall hunting is to locate a flock of birds, break them up and then come back later to call. The lost young birds respond readily to the call of the mother. You can use the same call that you use in the spring for gobblers—the yelp of the hen.

After turkeys there are black bear and wild boar. Both are scattered across America, but the true bear range is much larger. Most of the New England states, Maine, Massachusetts, New Hampshire, and Vermont, have huntable bear populations, particularly Maine where spring hunting over bait was popular for years. Bait is still permitted during a special late summer season, but spring hunting is a thing of the past. Not just in Maine, but all over the United States. Other northeastern bear hunting states include Pennsylvania and New York.

There is limited bear hunting in the South, but Georgia, North Carolina, South Carolina, Virginia, and West Virginia have bear populations and open seasons. Some of the best black bear hunting in America is found in eastern North Carolina near the coast.

The bear is not a critter of the plains and you do not find it in the Great Plains states, but the hunting is good in the border states of Michigan, Minnesota, and Wisconsin. To the south there is a good bear population in Arkansas.

Alaska is probably the best black bear hunting state in the United States, but it is too remote for an inexpensive hunt. Washington is a top bear hunting state and so are California and Oregon on the West Coast.

In the Rocky Mountain states you will find huntable bear populations in Arizona, Colorado, Idaho, Montana, Utah, and Wyoming. Black bears tend to take a back seat here, however, where the choices for big game hunting are many and other species are more attractive

Most of the bears in America are taken over bait or ahead of hounds, but many are also taken by still-hunting, much as you hunt deer, or from elevated stands. Bowhunters take a good number of bears from elevated stands, often

Black bears are found in many states both east and west of the Mississippi River.

while hunting for deer. So what approach is best for the novice bear hunter? Getting in on a hound bear hunt requires either signing up with a guide who uses dogs or finding a bear hunter who will allow you to join his hound hunts. Baiting is a more viable option, but except for a couple of New England states and Idaho and Montana in the West, hunting over bait is illegal. This pretty much eliminates this possibility for the majority of hunters.

Still-hunting is not nearly as effective as the other two methods, but it remains a possibility. Some scouting prior to a hunt to determine where bears are feeding and roaming will improve a hunter's chances of success.

Regardless of where you live in America, bear hunting is not far away. A single day of traveling will be sufficient in most cases. Bears are much closer for many hunters. A shiny black bear rug for your den or fireplace will mark you as a big game hunter—even if you never get another big game animal.

When the subject of wild boar hunting is brought up, thoughts swing immediately to the Great Smoky Mountains in western North Carolina and eastern Tennessee. Boar imported from the Ural Mountains of Russia and released there by a wealthy hunter many years ago have now spread throughout the rugged mountain country. Hunters from all over America have visited those mountains in quest of a wild boar—or more specifically a Russian wild boar. The hunting is still good there, but it's just the tip of the iceberg as far as wild boar hunting goes in America.

Before we go further let's settle a misconception about wild boars. Our domestic hog or swine was descended from the wild boar and the two are genetically the same. And neither is a native of America. The closest native pig we have is the little javelina of the Southwest, and it's distantly related at the best. Much of the wild boar population in the Great Smoky Mountains has been diluted by domestic hogs. Farmers in the foothills and valleys allow their swine to forage for themselves and they wander far up the mountain hollows to mate with the wild boars.

California, Florida, and Hawaii have healthy boar or hog populations that rival the famous wild boars of North Carolina and Tennessee. The ancestors of the California and Florida hogs were brought to this country by the Spanish explorers long before those Russian wild boars were released in North Carolina. I got a big old boar in Florida a few years ago that looks menacingly down at me from my office wall as I write this. He has vicious tusks and black wattles that drop from each side of his throat. His ancestors were undoubtedly brought to America from Europe by early Spanish explorers. That mount pretty well fulfills my desire for a wild boar.

Prior to writing a book called *Hunting Boar, Hogs, and Javelina* a few years ago, I surveyed wildlife agencies all over America in an effort to pin down the location of huntable wild boar populations. The results were surprising.

Wild boar, hogs, or pigs are genetically the same though called by different names. They are accessible throughout much of the United States and offer inexpensive big game hunting.

Alabama, Arkansas, California, Florida, Georgia, Hawaii, Louisiana, Mississippi, New Hampshire, North Carolina, Oregon, South Carolina, Tennessee, Texas, Virginia, and West Virginia all report the presence of wild boar or hogs, but the populations are very limited in several of them. In other states such as Michigan, New York, Ohio, and Pennsylvania wild boar hunting is offered on commercial hunting preserves. Hunting on some of these preserves can be very exciting and every bit as dangerous as is wild boar hunting wherever it is done. I hunted on a commercial preserve in Ohio and was very impressed with the quality of the hunting. The animals have keen senses of smell and while I was watching one group approach my stand, the wind switched to my back, carried my scent to the pigs, and they scattered like flushed turkeys.

A second look at that list of states reporting the presence of wild boar or hogs revealed the fact that the critters are considered game animals in California, Florida, Hawaii, North Carolina, Tennessee, and West Virginia. Generally these are also the states offering the best hunting. The hog is second in popularity only to the deer in California where the hog kill often exceeds that of the deer. Florida also provides an excellent opportunity to bag a boar or hog. The Hawaiian hogs are a mixture of animals brought from Europe and those brought to the islands by Polynesian people from other Pacific islands.

While they are not game animals in Georgia, Kentucky, Louisiana, Mississippi, South Carolina, and Texas, there is good hunting in all of these states and a high interest in it. Guided boar hunts are conducted in Georgia, and in Louisiana boar hunters have formed the Louisiana Wild Boar Association. Hunting them with hounds is popular in states where they are considered game animals as well as in those where they are not.

While boar or hogs can be taken ahead of hounds, this option is not readily available to the novice unless he lives in one of the states where this hunting method is popular and packs of hounds are kept and trained for that purpose. They can be hunted from stands as are bear and deer, and they can also be still-hunted. The critters often come out to feed late in the day and this is a good time to still-hunt for them. I took that Florida boar mentioned above while still-hunting late in the day.

A quick review of the states in which there is wild boar or hog hunting will tell you that the hunting is pretty well scattered across the United States, but more so across the southern part. Throw in the commercial hunting preserves and it becomes obvious that good wild boar hunting is seldom far away. Bear hunting may be a bit more available, but not much so.

Bear, boar, and turkeys, they can lead you well along the path to becoming a complete big game hunter—and the cost need not break your budget.

Chapter VI

Transportation… the Hunting Trio Approach

Transportation to and from a big game hunting area is a major cost in most hunting trips, but fortunately there are several ways to control it. The cost of gasoline for a South Dakota hunter going to Wyoming for an antelope hunt may not be much, but he should also factor in the wear and tear on his vehicle. It could be more than the outlay for gasoline. When one member of a hunting party furnishes the automobile he should be relieved of paying for the gasoline. The other members of the party can share that—and they may still come out ahead financially.

We will get into more detail on travel by automobile later, but first look at other possible means of transportation.

For distant trips, say a thousand miles or more, many hunters prefer flying. It's fast, saves a lot of time, and if you are on a tight time schedule it gives you more hunting time. Flying is probably the most expensive means of transportation you can use, and on unguided trips it means renting a car to get to and from your hunting grounds, an additional cost. Add to that the cost of shipping home the meat and antlers or the hide and flying becomes even more expensive.

Transporting firearms for air travel is no problem. Pack your guns in a hard case and check them through with your baggage. They'll be tagged and you have to certify that they are not loaded. I've never experienced problems with guns when flying, though an airlines clerk in Hawaii made me leave my ammo with her. I was flying from Honolulu to Hawaii, the Big Island, to hunt wild boar. "You can pick your ammunition up when you get back," she said. "Thanks. What good will it do me after the hunt?" This was an interisland airline, and it made no difference to her that I had checked my guns and ammunition through Dulles in Virginia and the airport in Los Angeles without a hitch. Such instances, however, are fortunately rare.

You can save on air transportation costs by avoiding peak times. Fly in the middle of the week, for example, instead of on weekends or holidays. You can also accumulate frequent flyer hours if your occupation involves flying. Or if on some trip your scheduled flight is overloaded, you might be offered a free flight anywhere in the United States if you will agree to take a later flight to help solve the airline's problem. A friend of mine uses an airlines credit card to make most of her purchases, and she accumulates points toward air fare. In fact she made a round trip to Spain with her accumulated points. You can also save transportation costs by flying with regional airlines. Airline rates are not regulated as they once were. There's a lot of competition out there. Take advantage of it and shop.

Travel by bus is less costly and modern buses are air conditioned and very comfortable. They travel through the night and you can get to a distant point much more rapidly than if you are traveling by private automobile. But you still have the cost of automobile rental at your destination. The same is true of trains, but in both cases you have to make arrangements for shipping your meat and trophy heads home. On my Hawaiian hunt I would have loved to bring home the wild boar, a big Rio Grand turkey gobbler, and some of the exotic gamebirds I took, but because I was traveling by air it was too much of a hassle—though I realize many hunters at least get their trophies home— probably by air express. And will you be able to rent a vehicle that will serve you on the hunting grounds? A 4x4 for example? Regardless of whether you travel by bus, plane, or train, the amount of luggage you carry with you is limited. Suppose you want to pack a complete camping outfit. Will any of these modes of travel permit it without a substantial additional cost?

I've never used a bus or train to reach my hunting destination, so I'm not speaking from experience. If that

A 4x4 vehicle that rides three comfortably and can be used off the road once in the hunting area is ideal for a cross-country trip by automobile.

mode of transportation suits your needs, check it out thoroughly and book your trip.

And that brings us to traveling by private vehicle. It's by far my favorite method. In the long run it's the least expensive—particularly if you can make up a small party of friends and share the cost.

To begin with there's the freedom this method puts into your hunting trip. You don't have to worry about making reservations, whether the plane will be on time, and meeting the scheduled departure either way, going or coming. Get your game early and you can pack up and head for home. No waiting around, killing time until your scheduled flight is due for departure.

And there is no limit on what you can carry with you, particularly if you drive a light pickup truck. Pack several of your favorite guns, a variety of clothing to meet changing weather conditions, and any other little items that add to the joy and success of a hunt. No weight limit. If necessary you can even rent a trailer to accommodate all of your gear and the meat and trophies you hope to bring home.

On such trips I like to drive my hunting vehicle which happens to be a 4x4 pickup truck at the present, though in the past I've driven an International Scout across country carrying a party of four. A little cramped perhaps, but not a real inconvenience. We towed a pop-up camping trailer which held part of our gear.

With the rising cost of gasoline I eventually sold the Scout which never got over 15 to 20 miles per gallon of gasoline and picked up a light truck which gets a healthy 30 miles to the gallon. The savings in gasoline costs is significant.

But best of all I like having my faithful and comfortable hunting vehicle in camp and on the hunting grounds. It's outfitted for hunting—a gun rack behind the seat, an ax, several knives, tow rope, jumper cables, flashlights, plenty of tools, a roll of paper towels, and toilet paper. My pickup body is covered with a cap with a lock which provides some security for the gear and other luggage in the body, but even more important, it offers protection from the weather. In a pinch I can park, roll out a sleeping bag and sleep in it. I know what the little truck is capable of, and I am much more comfortable with it than I would be with a rental car which may be entirely unsuited to hunting.

Before I embark on a cross country trip I take my vehicle in to my service man, tell him what I plan, and ask him to check it out thoroughly so as to avoid trouble on the highway. Following that procedure, I put over 200,000 trouble-free miles on my last Scout, and my present 4x4 pickup truck has 130,000 miles on it. Once it's checked out by my serviceman, I head out with confidence.

I live in Virginia on the East Coast and over the years I've made numerous trips west to the Rocky Mountain states to hunt. A trip by automobile from my home in central Virginia to the eastern slopes of the Rocky Mountains requires 36 hours or travel time. If I drive a normal eight to 10-hour day and spend the nights in a motel, that means two nights on the road and arrival late the third day—three days of traveling. Going and coming that means using up six days that I could be hunting. It also means motel costs for four nights. But look at it from another

While a vehicle can be used for cross-country travel, it should have a place to store rifles safely.

angle. By driving straight through I can leave my home early one morning, drive through the night, and be at my destination by sundown the second day. That eliminates the cost of spending four nights in motels—or any motel costs.

Traveling alone, as I have done too often perhaps, means skipping one night of sleep. Drinking a lot of coffee,

I can manage it—and at the worst suffer a little indigestion! Maybe it's holdover from my World War II combat experience with the Marines in the Pacific. Then we often went for days, napping 10 minutes or so when we could. I eat lightly. It helps keep me awake. On such trips my only stops are for meals, coffee, and gasoline. It's an inexpensive, highly efficient way to travel. Traveling at night means less traffic, though you will be surprised at how much there is on a modern interstate highway between midnight and dawn. Such travel is fascinating as well as cost effective.

A word of caution. If you get sleepy, stop, get out and walk around, drive with a window down to let in some fresh air, or even pull over at a convenient spot, lock your vehicle securely and get a quick nap. Don't risk falling asleep while driving. I reached this point once on a trip to Idaho for elk. I found a good pull-over spot already occupied by a couple of large trucks, but with plenty of room left for my little Scout. I shifted luggage around so I could stretch out, loaded up my Remington 700 30/06 and got in an hour or so of sleep. Well rested and alert, I eventually went on.

On a trip that stretches too deeply into the second night I check in at a motel and sleep soundly. I never drive through two nights in succession.

Traveling alone in this manner is acceptable, but I much prefer to have one or two hunting partners along. That way we can alternate at the driving and napping. Over the course of 36 hours you should be able to get in five or six hours of sleep. Some insist they can't sleep in a moving vehicle, but they will eventually. Their eyelids will get heavy, their head will nod, and suddenly they are snoring. Just don't reach this point while driving!

The ideal trip is one where there are a trio of hunters. One can drive, one can keep the driver awake through the night, and the other can sleep. They take turns, however, rotating between driving, riding shotgun, and sleeping. Two friends and I did this a few years ago on a trip to Newfoundland. A friend agreed to drive his pickup truck which has a roomy cab, plenty of room for the driver and two passengers

Over the years there have been drive-through-the-night trips to New Mexico for deer with four in the party—and a little cramped, a pair of us to Wyoming for antelope, and then another 3-party trip to Wyoming for antelope, a 3-party trip to North Dakota for huns and sharptailed-grouse, and others.

I like to travel by automobile watching the country pass by and trying to figure out what kind of hunting it offers, watching the sun set behind the prairie hills of Kansas and hours later watching it creep from behind a rugged mountain in the Rockies. About that time I begin looking for a good restaurant and breakfast. Well before dawn I may have stopped at a truck stop and enjoyed a chance conversation with fellow hunters. Some are headed out as I am, but others are headed home after a successful hunt. Many have animals strapped to the roofs of their vehicles, a practice which I discourage. The meat can pick up all kinds of highway odors which won't help it. Instead, put it inside the vehicle if at all possible and protect it. The body of a pickup truck with a cap on it is ideal. Some hunters have their meat processed at the site of the hunt and take it home in ice chests. Others quarter their animals and keep them cool in the unheated bed of the pickup truck. That's a major advantage of driving a pickup truck. The hunters can keep warm in the cab, but their meat will stay cool in the bed of the truck.

You get to appreciate America more when you travel by automobile. I do so when it is practical—which is true of most of my hunting trips.

It might be possible to rent pack horses for self-guided back country hunts.

Chapter VII

Running Your Own Hunt

A self-guided big game hunt, one that produces the game desired, is a highly rewarding effort. On guided hunts the hunter relies heavily upon the guide to put him within range of his game. His own expertise is all but reduced to making a clean shot and following up with a second one if necessary. The self-guided hunter on the other hand does it all, meaning he has to select a hunting area and plan his hunt so it will put him within bow or rifle range of his targeted game.

Self-guided hunts can be highly successful if planned and run properly. Otherwise they can be a complete flop. Success also varies according to the game sought. On western hunts antelope and mule deer are a reasonably sure bet, or draw a permit and a Maine moose shouldn't be too difficult. The most difficult part of a moose hunt is getting the big animal field dressed and back to your vehicle. This may mean quartering the animal and bringing it out a bit at a time. You will need help with this, though a party of two or three hunters should be able to handle it. Just keep this in mind when planning a hunt. On western antelope or mule deer hunts, however, it is often possible to drive your hunting vehicle to the site of the kill and simply load the game aboard. I've even been able to do this on a couple of elk hunts—drive right up to the downed animal.

You may be able to tow an ATV to your hunting area or drive a 4x4 vehicle with good clearance and the capacity to haul your animal out. A 4x4 pickup truck is an ideal vehicle for a self-guided hunt. You might be able to engage someone with pack horses, or rent a pack horse. In some instances you might be able to use a boat or canoe to get

The author took this nice New Mexico mule deer on a self-guided hunt.

the game out. The important thing here is to have a plan in place for getting your game from the site of the kill to your camp or quarters before you drop it with that well-placed shot. Don't kill the animal and then wonder how you are going to pack it out.

In planning a self-guided hunt the first thing to determine is what kind of game you want to hunt. The state-by-state, or province-by-province, list of big game in Chapter XVII will serve you in that respect. It at least narrows down your research to states and provinces where the game you seek is present. Beyond that the process becomes a bit more difficult.

Your first step is to contact those game or wildlife agencies and ask them for copies of their latest hunting regulations. Their addresses are given in Chapter XVI. The information will help you determine the dates of various seasons, information needed for planning vacation time. They will also give you the deadlines for applying for hunting permits. Today in most states the hunter has to enter his name in a lottery for drawing a permit for the major big game animals, particularly in the western United States. This is generally not the case for bear or boar hunting in the East.

Bit by bit the hunting regulations from the various agencies will arrive in your mail box, and you begin sorting out the possibilities. As you go through the process of elimination you will gradually build up information as to filing dates, seasons, and license costs. In most instances the regulations will give you the various game areas, and in some cases even harvest figures by area for the most recent season. That is the nugget of gold you need to plan a successful self-guided hunt. If that information is not included, get back to the agency of the state that seems most promising and ask for it. It is all but impossible to plan a self-guided hunt without this area-by-area harvest information. Without it, learning where the largest populations of animals are is all but impossible—unless you have a well-informed big game hunter to turn to.

Generally, the best choice of a hunting area is the one that produced the largest kill the most recent season. Don't stop there, however. Notice how many permits are available in each hunting area. Compare this information to the harvest information. You might find out that a hunting area with a smaller harvest might actually have a higher hunting success ratio. All you have to do is apply the number of permits against the harvest figures and determine the success ratio. The area with the smaller harvest might also be less crowded. This is the kind of information you can develop in the comfort of your living room.

Some hunt areas might allow either-sex hunting while in others male animals only are legal. Generally your chances of drawing a permit are higher where either-sex hunting is allowed. If you are willing to settle for a cow instead of a bull elk, for example, your chances of drawing a permit are higher than if you will accept a bull permit only.

A pair of deer hunters head back to camp with a nice buck.

Another often overlooked factor is that most self-guided hunters apply for hunt areas where there is an abundance of public land. There is usually a higher demand for permits in these areas. Your chances of being drawn are much higher in hunt areas where there is an abundance of private land. Keep that in mind when planning your hunt.

Some of the best big game hunting in North America is found on private land. This is not to say the public lands are not as good, but you are more likely to find them crowded. Pay a modest fee to hunt a ranch, and you may pretty much have the hunting area to yourself. Few ranchers are going to allow a crowd on their land regardless of the additional income it might provide. Over the years I've enjoyed good success hunting both private and public lands. In Chapter X "Second Class Guides" we will take a look at several ways of locating good private land to hunt. While we are on the subject, be sure to ask the agency to provide you with information on the available public lands. There might be a modest fee for this, particularly if the information needed includes good maps. Maps are a must if you plan to hunt public lands. You want to know where the boundaries are, otherwise you might end up on some landowner's property. An irate private landowner can be a problem to deal with—even if you do make an honest mistake.

National forest lands offer almost unlimited hunting opportunities in the western states and to a lesser degree elsewhere in America. If there are national forests in the state you plan to hunt, check out the location of the forest headquarters for addresses and telephone numbers. Contact those offices for maps. There may be a small fee for the maps, but it will be money well spent. Also check on the possibilities of state or province land such as state or provincial forests and public hunting areas. In Canada ask about Crown lands.

If you decide to go the private land way, then maps are unnecessary. The farmer or rancher will show you the boundaries to his property.

Accommodations, food and shelter, are serious considerations on a self-guided hunt. The hunter who does not eat well and get plenty of sleep isn't going to stay sharp very long. He may hold out for a day or so, but after that he tends to get sluggish and his senses become dull. Plan ahead for comfortable living conditions while on your hunt.

Camping is the least expensive way to live, and it will put you closer to your hunting area. Usually you can find good camping areas on the land you plan to hunt. A good hunting camp has a nearby source of clean drinking water, a ready source of firewood for cooking and heating, and the materials for erecting a pole to hang your game on. Select a campsite that is not subject to flooding. Camping near a stream with a large drainage area is always risky.

Getting a bull elk like this one out of back-country dictates some planning prior to the hunt.

Plan your meals before you leave home and pack the necessary ingredients to meet that plan. And be sure someone in the party is a reasonably good cook. Rotating cooks is a good idea if the party is large enough. This assures good meals and equal hunting time for all.

Motels in the vicinity of the hunting area are another possibility though this approach adds considerable expense to your hunt. The advantages are obvious—a comfortable bed and a hot shower to cap off a day of hunting. I've successfully hunted antelope, bear, boar, deer, and elk from a motel. You also need a good restaurant nearby if the motel doesn't have one. This should also be checked out prior to your hunt. Contact the tourist information office of the state or province you plan to hunt. The wildlife agency can furnish you with an address and telephone number. Make reservations before you leave home. Otherwise you might arrive at the site of your hunt and find all of the motels booked solid. This often occurs at the peak of the season in prime big game country.

If you go the motel route, you may run into a problem of caring for your game in the course of the hunt. You might luck out and find a motel that caters to hunters. If so

A bull moose can present a real logistics problem. Solve it before you hunt.

they may have facilities for hanging your game. Probably a better possibility is to locate a convenient meat processing plant you can turn your meat over to. We'll talk about handling your meat and getting it home in Chapter IX.

In some cases ranchers who list their lands with wildlife agencies for fee hunting also offer limited housing. Sometimes it may be nothing more than a crude shed which provides a roof overhead and a floor on which hunters can stretch out their air mattresses and sleeping bags. At the minimum most will allow you to camp somewhere on their lands.

Getting lost in strange wilderness country is always a possibility. This is a risk to prepare for on self-guided hunts. By all means carry a good compass. On guided hunts getting lost is rarely a risk, but if you are going to be in strange country for the first time prepare for the possibility. For one thing make a day pack part of daily equipment, just as much so as your rifle and ammunition. Include in that pack such things as a first aid kit, plenty of matches in a waterproof box, some quick-energy foods such as granola bars, water purification tablets, and a light space blanket to serve as a temporary shelter or ground cover should you have to spend the night out. Your hunting knife becomes increasingly valuable. With a good fire to keep you warm, and a shelter to keep you dry, you can get by for several days with a minimum of food—just enough to ward off hunger.

You and your hunting partners should have in place a plan should one member of the party get lost and not arrive back at a designated time. Basically, all this means is having at least one member of the party knowing the general area in which you will be hunting.

Self-guided hunts obviously take many forms, but it is the way the vast majority of hunters seek their game. Over almost a lifetime of hunting all over America I've seen hunting camps in a great variety of good game country. Often there has been a bear, boar, deer, elk, or some other big game animal hanging on an improvised game pole and a campfire blazing or smoldering in a ring of stones collected on the spot. That to me is American big game hunting at its best—hunters successfully running their own show. There is no better test of the true hunter.

Chapter VIII

Drop Hunts

A drop hunt is a more ambitious self-guided hunt in that the hunter or hunters engage some kind of transportation to get to and from the hunting area. Once there the hunter runs his own hunt, just as described in Chapter VII, "Running Your Own Hunt," though his two feet might be the only means of transportation on the hunting grounds.

A drop hunt is an inexpensive way to enjoy a back country or wilderness hunt, but it is not for the inexperienced. Still, anyone who has done some camping and successfully hunted more accessible big game such as bear, boar, or deer should experience no problems—provided he takes the necessary precautions.

Let's take for example a wilderness hunt in Alaska that my wife and I enjoyed a few years ago. We spent the summer camping in the 49th state that year, taking the ferry up from Prince Rupert, British Columbia, and traveling home down the famous Alaska Highway. It was a once-in-a-lifetime trip, but I did more fishing than hunting.

One thing I wanted to do before leaving this beautiful and unique state was take a black bear. The season wasn't open on grizzly bears while we were there, nor on any game to speak of. I did take a few snowshoe hares with my .22 caliber rifle and we feasted on them in camp. In much of the state there was no closed season on black bears, however. At that point in my life I had taken a number of North American big game animals so had the hunting experience. My wife and I had been camping for years, and in fact had been camping in Alaska for over a month, so we had no qualms about wilderness camping and hunting.

Despite my efforts I was having trouble getting that black bear. Then I ran into a fellow outdoor writer and

Arrange for a bush pilot to drop you off and come back for you at the end of your hunt.

hunting guide whom I knew by reputation. He also recognized my name from bylines in hunting magazines. Originally from the Midwest, he now lived in Alaska, writing and doing some guiding. "Why don't you go down to Seward. There's a little airport there and you can get them to fly you down to the Prince William Sound area where there is an abundance of bears," he suggested when I mentioned my desire to get an Alaskan black bear.

With that information Ginny and I broke camp and headed south to Seward. We located the tiny airport without difficulty and booked one of the pilots to fly us to our chosen location. "There's a tiny lake there we land on, but the weather is not suitable for flying at the moment. Why don't you camp close by and stand by." We located a convenient campground and set up our little pop-up Apache camping trailer which we had been living in since leaving Virginia over a month earlier.

While waiting we shopped for groceries for the trip. The pilot owned a little cabin on the lake and that would be our home while there. We were planning for a one week's stay, plenty of time to take a bear. "Take supplies sufficient for 10 days," he told us, "in the event the weather is such that I can't get back to you at the end of the week."

We checked in at the airport daily and were finally advised that the weather problem had passed and we could fly. He was flying a small amphibious plane. We took off from the airport on wheels, but used the pontoons to put down on the lake. The lake drained a glacier, and a small stream connected it with the sound, a short distance away. "Good salmon fishing," he said pointing to the stream as we circled to land.

The cabin wasn't much, but it was screened in for protection from mosquitoes and had a wood cooking stove, bunks, and even a small supply of food left by the last occupant. We didn't know it then, but that bit of leftover staples would keep us going before the trip was over.

There were black bears in every direction, but they gave the cabin a wide berth, though we did awake one night to find one rummaging near the cabin. The fishing was also fabulous, and I divided my time between fishing and hunting bears. There were also three little Alaska Sitka deer that hung out nearby, but the season wasn't open on them yet. Had it been I could have taken one easily.

We had absolutely no contact with the outside world, a fact that gave us some concern. "There are a couple of flags in the cabin," explained the pilot. "If you have a serious emergency put out the red one where it can be seen from the air. Any pilot that sees it will put down, leave his passengers there temporarily, and fly you in. If you put out the white flag, he will put down and bring instructions to me that you want to come in. Make sure he gets your name." That was some consolation, but there were several stormy days when no one was flying. But given the weather, the system would work. We found out by accident. I was cleaning salmon one bright morning in front of the cabin and took off my red shirt and hung it on a bush. Soon thereafter I realized that a plane was circling overhead preparatory to landing. It suddenly dawned on me that my red shirt had his attention. I straightened up from cleaning salmon and waved him off.

We did run into a problem, however, for which there was no immediate solution. On the day our pilot was to pick us up a real storm blew in and it rained and the wind

Maybe you would like a Packer to transport you in on his horses and return for you at the end of your hunt.

blew for three days. No planes were flying. They couldn't. Finally our food ran out and we dug into the staples left there by a previous tenant, primarily macaroni. We also ate a lot of salmon, and I was seriously considering shooting one of the Sitka deer, report it later and pay whatever penalty I was assessed.

It was still heavily overcast and raining on and off one morning when we heard a plane nearby. We shouted for joy when our pilot circled overhead and put down on the lake. I've seldom been more overjoyed to see someone.

That experience serves to illustrate graphically what we mean when we talk about drop hunts. In this instance the pilot knew where we would find good bear hunting and he had the means to get us there and drop us off. The hunting would then be my responsibility. No guide to help locate the game and look over my shoulder when I shot. It was truly a self-guided hunt once we got there. The pilot charged us $200 for the transportation and the week in his cabin. The fee also included hauling back any fish and game we wanted to keep. Had we booked a guide in addition, the fee would have been considerably more. The bear hunting and the salmon fishing were fabulous, and later when the seasons opened the same setup was available for Sitka deer and the mountain goats. The goats ranged a nearby mountain across the lake.

I would have felt better if we could have maintained radio contact with the little Seward airport from which we flew. That's something to consider on drop hunts. Had we had an emergency during those days the planes were not flying, we could have had a serious problem. The flag system worked, but only when the conditions were right for flying.

Drop hunts by plane are a possibility only when there is water or a landing strip of some kind in the vicinity of the area you plan to hunt. Alaska bush pilots are also good at putting their little planes down on beaches or other suitable landing areas, but they are not always available. Water is usually available in the lake country of Canada and a few northern states such as Maine or Minnesota. That's one reason you see so many bush planes in Canada and in some parts of the northern United States. You rarely see them in the big game country of the western states where packing in by horses is so popular.

In preparing for a drop hunt, pack camping gear, food, and other supplies just as if you were going to drive into back country and set up a hunting camp. The big difference is that you are stranded for the designated time. You live, eat, and sleep on what you have with you, though in an emergency you could build additional shelter from native materials and supplement your meals with fish, game, and edible plants. Plants, however, are not usually available during the fall hunting season.

Try to anticipate all of your needs, make a list, and check it thoroughly. Go properly prepared and your drop hunt will come off as a highly rewarding experience.

I suspect the bush plane is the vehicle used on most drop hunts. The major reason is that it can land on water, and that is the most available landing strip in most wilderness country. When selecting a pilot check out his references. You don't want one who flies by the seat of his pants as the expression goes. You don't want an equipment failure, nor do you want a pilot who is so unreliable he might not pick you up at the appointed time—or worse yet—not at all! Ideally you should be able to maintain radio contact with the outside world throughout your hunt. This is particularly valuable in the case of an emergency, a heart attack for example.

In the western United States pack horses are the more customary vehicle to get hunters into back country. You arrange with someone who owns pack horses to pack you and your equipment into back country and return to pick you up later. In some cases 4x4 vehicles may be used over rough jeep trails for the same purpose. There is also the possibility of transportation by canoe or boat. A friend and I had a marina operator transport us across Fontana Lake in the rugged mountains of western North Carolina. Across the lake were the famous Great Smoky Mountains, true wilderness country, much of which was in the Great Smoky Mountains National Park. While the park was off limits to hunting, there was then a sizable chunk of wilderness that bordered the lake that was open to hunting black bears and wild boar. A wild boar was our goal. Except by boat the only way to reach that wilderness country was on foot. That meant packing in our camping gear which would not have been too much of a problem except for the time it consumed. Getting a couple of big old boars out would have been a problem, and the marina operator solved that for us. We could drag them to the lake and he would pick them up in one of his boats.

Drop hunts take many forms when it comes to selecting the kind of transportation needed to transport you and your camping gear in and pick it up later when hopefully you will also have game to get out. In the simplest form you select a hunting area you are interested in based on research developed as outlined in Chapter VII "Running Your Own Hunt," and then find someone, a bush pilot, someone who owns horses, or someone with a suitable boat to provide the transportation to get you and your equipment in and out. Our Fontana Lake hunt is a good example. I'm not sure the marina operator had ever done that before, but he had the means to do so and we recognized it.

On a more formal basis there are outfitters for whom drop hunts are a major part of their business. They not only furnish transportation, but also complete camping equipment, often including carefully selected groceries, and can even suggest a good hunting area which they can get you to. Some even have camps already set up, or crude cabins as did our Alaskan bush pilot. Others may help you set up camp before they leave you.

The fees vary considerably, of course, depending upon what services are provided. In any event a drop hunt is considerably less expensive than a completely guided one.

Locating drop hunt services may take a little investigation. Check with the state or provincial wildlife agencies. If they can't provide you with possibilities maybe they can refer you to someone who can, the local tourism office for example. You can also call outfitters or bush plane pilots who advertise in outdoor magazines.

A drop hunt is an excellent and inexpensive way to get into top big game country.

If you are experienced in handling horses you might be able to rent horses to pack you and your outfit in.

Chapter IX

Reaching Remote Country on Your Own

Most of us can hunt bear, boar, deer, turkeys, and often other big game without having to make a long trip. In some cases almost in our backyards. Seldom do we venture far into the back country or true wilderness. That's not bad. There is some amazingly good hunting on the very heels of civilization, hunting that rarely makes a big dent in your budget. If that's all you can afford, don't feel bad about what life has dealt you. You will find some of the best big game hunting in America within a couple of hours' drive of many major cities. And hunters who take bear, boar, or deer with any regularity can hold their own with just about any big game hunter in America, regardless of how impressive his trophy room might be.

But for those who harbor a yen to get into back country for elk, goats, moose, or other big game, there are ways to do it own your own. Doing so, however, will require a fair amount of research regarding the game and country you plan to hunt, and also a good deal of organization and preparation.

I know some excellent white-tailed deer hunters who have never owned a compass or referred to a map of the area they hunt. They need neither. They know their hunting country well, and you couldn't lose them if you tried. But venturing into the wilderness or back country with which they are unfamiliar is an entirely different challenge. Their hunting expertise will serve them well on such trips, but they need to develop new skills for traveling virgin territory or wilderness.

Were you a Boy Scout in your youth? Did you learn to read a map and use a compass. If so brush up on those skills. You will need them on a wilderness hunt—particularly a trip into roadless back country. Don't take this advice lightly. A working knowledge of a compass and maps could mean the difference between a successful hunting trip and one that can only be described as a flop. It could even be the difference between life and death.

The first step in planning a wilderness hunt is to contact the game agency of the state or province you want to hunt and develop the information on the location of game populations. Proceed just as described in Chapter VIII "Running Your Own Hunt." The more general range of the animal you want to hunt can be determined generally by referring to Chapter XVII "State and Provincial Listing of Big Game." This narrows down your search considerably. You can immediately eliminate Alabama, for example, for mountain goats! With the hunting area established, you want to get topographical maps of the area. The state or provincial game agency may be able to supply them, but if not they can direct you to a source. There are available both commercial and government topographical maps of just about every section of the United States and Canada.

Spend some hard study time on that map or maps. Familiarize yourself with all of the prominent terrain features such as mountain peaks, lakes or ponds, fire towers, streams—anything that will help you orient yourself once you are in your hunting area.

With good hunting territory located as described in Chapter VII "Running Your Own Hunt," you are ready to begin making plans. The game is there, but how are you going to get back there and hunt it? The region is an untracked wilderness. You could have someone drop you off and pick you up at the end of the hunt. This possibility was described in Chapter VII "Drop Hunts," but you can't afford it or prefer not to add on that expense. You also want to do your own thing.

We're talking about wilderness travel and you probably have a choice of several means of transportation—your own two feet, a canoe or boat, horseback, and possibly an

ATV or 4x4 vehicle. The latter depends upon the availability of trails or possibly logging roads.

Let's take a look at boats or canoes first. Watercraft for some reason seems to have a good deal of appeal. Maybe it's because the Indians and early explorers used that method often for getting beyond the fringes of civilization. They used nature's own roads, the waterways.

In my own mind the ideal setup for a self-run wilderness hunt is a vast wilderness region through which a major river or stream flows. Ideally that stream has good access upstream just outside of the wilderness region and a good takeout point once you leave the wilderness area. There are such areas around the United States, but probably more so in Canada.

One American possibility I know of is the combination of the Greenbrier River and the Monongahela National Forest in West Virginia. A canoe can put a pair of hunters in wilderness country and hunting for bear, deer, and turkeys. I'm not necessarily recommending this trip. Just using it as an example of the possibilities our streams offer us. You don't have to seek wilderness areas for bear, deer, and turkeys, but some hunters like to get into back country just for the experience. It also offers better opportunities for trophy animals.

Having located the combination of big game and wilderness you prefer, a good topographical map becomes one of your most valuable tools. Use it to study the part of the wilderness area the river will take you to. Of particular importance is a thorough study of the river itself. Does it have good access just outside of the wilderness area? Points where you can launch your canoe or boat and later take it out? You'll have to set up some kind of shuttle so that you can return quickly to the launching area to pick up your vehicle. The map should answer that for you. Even more important is the nature of the stream. Does it have a lot of fast water you may be hesitant to tackle? Study the contour lines. Are there points where they are very close together where they cross the river? If so you've located some fast water. Does the map indicate portage trails around the fast water?

The map should also tell you whether a particular section of the river is flowing through a deep gorge. If so, you may want to avoid planning on camping there. It could mean pulling your camping gear, guns, and other equipment up a steep cliff. You might leave your boat or canoe on the banks of the stream, but there is always the risk of a flash flood sweeping them away. Again study the contour lines. If they are close together along a river, it almost certainly means the river is running through a deep gorge. Pick a more gentle slope to the stream for your hunting camp.

Once you have become thoroughly familiar with the stream from your map study, check out your conclusions with someone who is familiar with the area. This could be a forest ranger who works the area, canoe outfitters who launch their clients on the river, canoe club members, or even the company or agency from whom you purchased the topographical map.

The selection of a boat or canoe for the trip should be given some deep thought. Remember that in addition to carrying you, your hunting partners, and all the gear you need for living a week or 10 days away from civilization it should be roomy enough to carry out your game. Whether you choose a canoe or john boat will depend much upon the nature of the river. Portaging a heavy john boat around some dangerous rapids could be a burden. On the other hand a john boat will be roomy with ample space for plenty of camping and hunting gear and game. Will you need an outboard motor? Again, much will depend upon the river. If the river has a good current that will carry you along, there should be little need for a motor.

Water offers a number of options for reaching back country. If a river flowing through or into a wilderness area does not have a number of fast rapids, you can load up an outboard-powered boat and make your run into good hunting country and then return by the same route. In such cases if the river permits it I would prefer to motor upstream instead of down. The reason is simple. If the motor conks out and you have to eventually row or paddle back to your starting point it will be much easier to do so going downstream with the current.

In many parts of the country you can reach back country on a lake. Many lakes have civilization on one side and wilderness on the other. Earlier I mentioned North Carolina's Fontana Lake. A guide took us across the lake to the Great Smoky Mountains and many square miles of wilderness on the far side. We could have actually launched our own boat or used a rental boat and saved a guide's fee. The guide's knowledge of the country, however, saved us doing a lot of map study and planning which would have been required had we decided to go on our own. In other words the guide already knows much about the country you plan to hunt, knowledge that you could otherwise acquire only by research and study of maps. That's a major difference between a guided hunt and a self-guided one. You have to take the time to acquire the knowledge the guide already has. That is much of what you pay him for.

If you are in good physical condition and have the time to do so, your own two feet can get you just about anywhere you want to go in back country or a wilderness area. There are limitations, of course, limitations on how much gear you can pack on your back, and even more serious limitations on your capability of packing out a sizable game animal, a 1,000-pound bull moose for example.

If you strike out across untracked wilderness, a compass becomes a priceless piece of equipment. When I was going through officer's candidate school at the Marine Corps Base in Quantico, Virginia, a number of years ago, part of our program included a compass march. We were taken several miles from our barracks on a dark, moonless night, given a compass and an azimuth, and told to find our way back to the barracks through a virtual wilderness area. A friend and I teamed up. Since I seemed to have had more experience with the compass, I took the instrument and we started for home. I would take a compass reading and locate some distinctive terrain feature such as a dead tree on the horizon and my friend would take off to that point. Once I joined him, I would take another reading, locate a prominent feature, and we would repeat the procedure. We arrived back at headquarters in good time, being the second team to check in. That is a good example of how a compass should be used in wilderness travel. The ability to read a topographical map and use a compass will keep a hunter from becoming hopelessly lost.

Another way to get safely into and out of a wilderness area is to take a stream and follow it to its headquarters—and then follow it out when you are ready to move. Streams follow valleys so the hiking should be easier, and game animals like valleys and a ready source of water.

Packing out game, particularly sizable animals is a real problem, and the best way to do this is to quarter the animal or animals and spread the load among all hunters on the trip. It may even mean making a return trip to get the game out. Give this plenty of thought before you drop a big animal miles from the nearest road or body of water.

Packing in by horseback is another possibility—provided you own a horse or can borrow or buy the temporary use of one. You also need some ability to handle horses and keep them fed and healthy in camp. Horses are best used on trails of which there are many in most wilderness areas. You can travel farther and faster by horseback, carry more equipment than you can by backpacking, and have the horse to pack out your game at the end of the hunt.

Four-by-four vehicles with good clearance or ATV's are another possibility for getting into back country, but at the minimum you will need a good trail. ATV's can go where the average 4x4 cannot. Many public lands have a set policy on the use of motorized vehicles. Check carefully on this. In many regions horses can be use where 4x4s and ATVs are prohibited. If you use either vehicle be sure you pack enough gasoline to get you in and out and to handle the use of the vehicle while in a hunting camp.

An ATV might be the answer to reaching back country on your own.

I enjoy handling 4x4 vehicles and am now well into my fourth one. It's amazing what these vehicles can do. They are a real asset on any hunt, wilderness or otherwise.

Transportation to and from a back country hunting camp is a major consideration. Give it plenty of thought and consider carefully the several options.

Chapter X

Second Class Guides

Guiding big game hunters is a booming business today. Not just in America, but pretty much all over the world where desirable big game animals live. Many people, those who enjoy the outdoors, make a good living from guiding hunters. Any number of modern hunters wouldn't think of going on a big game hunt without a guide. And for a good reason. The success ratio for guided hunts is high—much more so than for those where a guide is not employed.

Good guides are professionals. They know the country and the game they hunt—and they know hunters. Season after season they deal with all kinds—novices on their first big game hunts, well-experienced hunters whose trophy rooms attest to their ability as well as their experience, young hunters, old hunters, healthy hunters, and others whose health problems require adjustments from the norm. A good guide earns his money. He or she is worth every penny you pay for the many services he offers. A good guide is also the surest route to success.

But the top, well-known guides are expensive. Their fees are beyond the budgets of a great many wanna-be big game hunters. They have to cover advertising in the major outdoor magazines, booths at numerous outdoor shows across the country, and booking fees if they use hunting services whose sole business is putting hunters and competent guides together. They may also have to provide bush plane services, a string of horses including pack animals and riding horses for their hunters, camping equipment, possibly boats or canoes, and a staff that includes a cook and often several assistant guides. They also have to factor in a decent profit for their efforts. Guiding is a business with overhead costs just as any other enterprise.

Fortunately, throughout the major big game hunting regions of America there are those that hunters and outdoor writers often refer to as second-class guides. "Second class" probably does them an injustice, even though it is a common term. They are as a class good hunters first and guides second. Rarely is guiding their primary source of income. Many work at logging and lumbering, ranching, farming, or some other occupation that keeps them in touch with the country they hunt. Many are firemen, law enforcement officers, teachers, and so on.

Second class guides do not advertise or visit outdoor shows. They build a business mostly through word of mouth. Their outlays for equipment are minimal. Most limit themselves to hunting gear they have accumulated over the years in pursuit of their personal hunting interests. Hunting, farm, or ranch vehicles may serve as field transportation. The same is true of horses and camping gear—if they are needed. Most seem to limit their guiding efforts to game and territory that does not require camping.

In some instances bear, boar, and deer hunting is done with hounds, and if you can find a guide who hunts with a club that owns hounds, you may have uncovered a rare opportunity.

Thinking back over many years of hunting I recall a Newfoundland moose guide who worked in a logging camp most of the year, and another Newfoundland guide who got me within easy rifle range of a woodland caribou but spent most of the year as a commercial fisherman. There was the Texas state trooper who guided me on a highly successful white-tailed deer hunt, and the Wyoming rodeo rider who helped me find an antelope. A Quebec timber company appraiser took a few days off each season to guide black bear hunters, and I was one of his many successful hunters.

The availability of second class guides depends much upon the kind of game you hunt. Finding such a guide for antelope, black bear, mule and white-tailed deer, and wild boar is easier than finding one for elk, goats, grizzly bears, moose, and sheep for example. The more remote the game the less likely are your chances of locating a good second class guide to serve you on your hunt. Most second class guides simply do not have the equipment and time for such hunting trips, many of which may stretch into several weeks.

Another advantage a second class guide often offers is access to private land. Typically local hunters who have lived in a community for years have been able to gradually gain access to many acres of private land for their personal hunting. It may be a ranch, farming land, timber land, or other private holdings owned by a friend or neighbor who allows a few friends or neighbors to hunt. That alone, access to good hunting land, is well worth the modest fees that second class guides charge. Taking other hunters on such land is something they have to handle with care. Few landowners want to provide lands for guided hunts—or commercial hunting. Your guide may have made specific arrangements to do so, or he may simply take you as a friend.

It is possible, of course, that your second-class guide has secured hunting rights to a piece of choice property by buying or leasing them. Leasing may mean no more than paying the property taxes. Some farmers and ranchers with substantial land may offer their own services as guides. Regardless of the arrangement, if the guide has access to good private hunting land he has a lot to offer in addition to his grasp of the local game picture and how to approach it.

Because these second class guides do not advertise in the major national outdoor magazines, locating them can be a problem. They are out there, available, and probably have some open dates, but if you don't know about them their services are of little value. I suppose over the years many hunters have located excellent second-class guides by word of mouth. A local hunter returns from a successful hunting trip and he is anxious to tell his friends about it. The friend is impressed and gets the guide's telephone number or address and sets up a hunt of his own. Of the various ways of locating a second class guide, this is probably by far the best. You spend a minimum of time searching for the guide you want, but best of all you have immediately solved the question of credibility. Your friend enjoyed a fine hunt and has no reservations about recommending his guide. You have the word of a trusted friend to rely upon.

A good example of this is an antelope hunt some friends and I enjoyed in Wyoming a few years ago. We had obtained the guide's name from a list furnished us by the Wyoming Game and Fish Department. I later recommended him to a fellow church member who was interested in an antelope hunt. He called and booked a hunt. Later in the year, when the antelope season had opened, he and a friend and their wives drove west on a fall vacation and part of that vacation was a successful hunt with the guide I recommended. No doubt they will somewhere down the pike recommend the guide to other friends, and the Wyoming guide's business will grow.

Unfortunately, such a casual lead is not always present and the search for an inexpensive guide is necessary. Where do you begin?

Do you belong to a hunting club? Are there among the members someone who has hunted with the kind of guide you seek? Does the club have a newsletter where you can run an appeal for help? Do you belong to a national organization that has hunters among its membership? If they live in the part of the country you want to hunt, call or write them and ask for recommendations. Maybe you work for a national organization and in the course of your daily work you are in contact with fellow employees in the country you are interested in. The next time you are on the telephone ask them about the possibility. It's a small world we live in today and communication with hunters around the country is no problem. Write, call, go on-line.

Probably the surest approach, however, is provided by the state game or wildlife agencies in the states you are interested in. In states with healthy big game populations and where guiding is a big business, the agencies often license guides.

This is usually a precautionary measure to protect the public. Guides applying for licenses may be required to pass some kind of test to help assure their competency. In other words before someone can offer his services as a guide he must be licensed. If this list is available to the public, ask for it and you have a ready reference. Even in states where guides are not required to be licensed, the wildlife agencies often maintain a list of individuals who guide hunters. They do so primarily to be able to provide this information to hunters looking for guide service.

For obvious reasons the agencies cannot recommend a specific guide. In other words they cannot risk being biased or showing favoritism. And unfortunately, even among the licensed guides there are some bad eggs. Sifting them from your prospect list becomes your responsibility. Often you can size them up on the telephone. Does the guide you have called come on too strong, painting glowing pictures of the game available? Does he oversell his services? Or does he come across with what you consider the true facts? Does he appear to tell it as it is? "Sure we've got some nice muley bucks, but they are not always easy to hunt. I can't guarantee you a trophy." That's the kind of guide I like to talk to.

But don't rely too heavily upon your ability to size someone up on the telephone, or through his letters. Ask for a couple of references. If he balks, politely thank him and go on to the next guide on your list. A good guide who has a long list of satisfied clients isn't going to hedge on his references. In fact he will readily supply them. Call a couple of the references he supplies and you should have a good idea of what kind of person you are doing business with.

Second class guides offer a wide variety of services. I talked to one western guide a few years ago who in addition to guiding also furnished a heated shed or Appalachian Trail type shelter. As I recall all was included in his modest fee. I didn't take him up for the simple reason that the type of hunting I was looking for was not particularly good in his area. I thanked him, made a note, and suggested it was very possible that I would be back in touch with him later. I haven't yet, but I still have his name and telephone number.

In some cases second class guides may offer to put you up in their homes. An Arizona javelina guide did that for me a few years ago. I wasn't there long enough to be an imposition on his family. I got my animal early the first day out and then headed for home. In some cases they may set up tent hunting camps for their hunters and leave them up for the season.

Probably the more usual setup, however, is for the guide to provide guiding service only. He may pick you up at your motel and drop you off later in the day. You eat at a convenient restaurant and probably have them pack you a lunch. Most guides will take care of field dressing your animal and transporting it to a local meat processor if you don't have your own transportation.

Those so-called "second class" guides send home thousands of happy hunters every hunting season, and they do so at a cost that does not put a big dent in the family budget. They're hunters at heart and they enjoy hunters who are kindred souls. Over the years some of my most memorable big game hunts have been the product of second class guides who work hard for their hunters.

Chapter XI

Swap a Hunt

At an ambitious family reunion, an attempt to gather the scattered clan from around the globe, you meet a distant cousin and make feeble attempts to start a conversation. The going is tough. But then you happen to mention that you are a deer hunter and suddenly his eyes light up. The pace picks up noticeably, and before you know it genealogy and attempts to figure out how you are related are forgotten. You have a stronger bond. You are both big game hunters.

If you have some good hunting or fishing on tap you might be able to swap a hunt and enjoy this kind of elk hunting.

The time passes rapidly as you talk avidly about hunting experiences, rifles, blackpowder, bowhunting, and hunting trips you hope to take. The kind of things hunters talk about wherever and whenever they meet—common ground. He's from Oregon, across the country from your home in the East, but he's a deer hunter also. The difference is that he hunts black-tailed deer found along the Pacific coast and you are a whitetail hunter. You compare notes, and before you know it you have an invitation to come west and enjoy his kind of hunting. You agree to do so on the condition that he come east and allow you to show him some exciting white-tailed deer hunting. In other words you swap hunts.

The beauty of this arrangement is that you both have uncovered hunting guides who are probably as good or better than any you could engage professionally and pay a substantial fee. He has taken countless little black-tailed deer, knows his hunting territory as he does the back of his hand, and may have access to some prime private land. In other words he is on top of his black-tailed hunting, up on the latest regulations, and is thoroughly familiar with the habits and characteristics of the animal you will hunt. You couldn't ask for a better setup. Your side of the bargain is to return the favor by showing him the very best white-tailed deer hunting you can find. Take him onto prime private land if you can. Don't worry about giving away the secret to your favorite hunting spot. After all he's going to hunt it only once. Oregon is too far away for him to become a regular.

Treat your swap-a-hunt partner as the guest he is. See that he sleeps well and enjoys your home-cooked meals. When he kills his deer pitch in and help him field dress it and drag it to your vehicle. Take the critter to your favorite butcher if you don't normally do your own butchering. If he has bagged a trophy recommend a reliable taxidermist. Hopefully, your swap-a-hunt partner will treat you the same way.

You also owe it to your partner to brush up on the blacktail deer, learn as much as you can about it, how it is hunted, the animal's habits, and the kind of country and cover it prefers. Read up on the hunting regulations and make sure you don't miss the deadline for filing for a license—if there is a deadline. This is fairly common in the West. Do your homework and you will enjoy your hunt more, and your partner will respect you as an equal.

As a host keep in mind that your guest may or may not have had the opportunity to brush up on the hunting regulations of what is a strange state to him. Make sure he is properly licensed and complies with regulations on checking in or reporting his kill. If he has to file early for his license, make sure that he is aware of this.

Seasons may determine who runs the first hunt. Generally West Coast deer seasons begin in August or September whereas most Eastern seasons don't open until November or December. There are exceptions, but that is the general pattern. Chances are your distant cousin, now a close hunting friend, will host you before you can host him. In other words, being an Easterner you will be a guest first. That's an advantage. He can set the pace, giving you some idea as to what your swap-a-hunt partner will expect when it's your time to be the host. But remember that being a proper guest can be just as demanding as being a good host. You will have to respect each other's time schedule, families, and other personal responsibilities.

In some cases it may be advisable to stay in a nearby motel rather than upset the tight routine that so many modern families live with. Both parents might work, for example, and youngsters have to be shuttled to and from day-care centers or school.

On the other hand if you are both retired, the picture clears considerably. There is plenty of room for adjustments in daily routines.

A family reunion is probably not a good example of ways to meet hunters from other parts of the country, though these new contacts come in many different ways, ways we would probably never think of. You just might be talking to a salesman visiting your office or home and uncover a hunter from a distant state. On a business or pleasure trip you might chance upon such hunter. He may be seated beside you on a plane. A chance conversation in the lobby of a hotel or motel might give the chance you need. The possibilities are just about endless.

A few years ago a reader in California picked up a copy of one of my bird hunting books. Somehow he got my address and wrote me. He was coming to Virginia on a Christmas vacation and wanted to hunt bobwhite quail for a day or so. Could I help? I assured him I would try, though the quail hunting was poor that year. He rented a car and arrived early one morning following directions that I had given him. I loaded up my two English setters and we hit the fields, managing to pick up a few birds and get some good work from my setters. That was his primary interest because pointing dogs are not often used for the western quail he hunts most of the time. My wife served a hot lunch and he departed late in the day with a good grasp of bobwhite quail. He enjoyed the hunt and so did I. I bid him goodby with an open invitation to visit him in California and hunt valley quail. So far I haven't taken advantage of that generous invitation, but it's definitely on my agenda.

Incidental opportunities are always a possibility, but there are quicker and more direct methods. Planned approaches that go directly to the heart of setting up swap-a-hunts.

One good one is the North American Hunting Club headquartered in Minnesota. Among membership benefits is a national hunting magazine, and among the features in the magazine is a monthly listing of swap hunt listings of members. It works this way. A member of the organization is interested in a particular kind of hunt in a particular kind of country. Next he has to decide what he has to offer, and then he sends in his request for listing.

For his own hunt, the one on which he will be the guest, he may specify time or other specifics, whether or not he will fly and need field transportation, or motel reservations if he prefers that kind of accommodations, and so on. Let your prospective host know exactly what you are looking for. The simpler you can keep your needs, the better are your chances of finding a swap-a-hunt partner. "I can sleep anywhere—on a sofa, in a hunting camp, in the open in a sleeping bag, the body of a pickup truck," so on. That makes it easier for a prospective host. It also tells him you are a pretty regular guy and will not be overly demanding.

Now what do you have to offer? Something that will hold appeal for a hunting partner? You can begin by considering what kind of hunting he has available to him in his home territory. An Alabama hunter isn't going to be overly excited about a white-tailed deer hunting trip to Virginia, but he might like a chance at one of those trophy bucks that Maine is noted for. If you own or have access to a hunting lodge or camp, that might make your listing more attractive.

Over the years I have noticed that Midwestern hunters who also fish are often interested in coming to Virginia for some good saltwater fishing. It's something not available to them locally. Do you have a fishing boat that will handle the briny waters, and are you adept at boat handling? Maybe it even has a cabin and you can spend several days aboard. Western hunters seem to have a particular interest in hunting bobwhite quail on an Old South plantation. It's something they have read about so much, but never experienced. The Old South, big plantations, classy pointing dogs, horse or mule-drawn field transportation, dog handlers—an atmosphere fanned by stories in numerous magazines. They would like a taste of it.

Midwestern hunters have good hunting for the likes of hun, pheasants, and sharptail grouse. Offer that to an Eastern hunter and he might put you on a trophy old white-tailed buck. Western hunters, those living in the Rocky Mountains region have a variety of big game to offer in exchange for hunting experiences they know of only from the pages of outdoor magazines.

Use your imagination. Decide what you are particularly interested in hunting, and then consider what you have to offer in exchange. Don't overlook unique fishing opportunities. Most hunters are also avid anglers.

The North American Hunting Club is probably as good an opportunity as you will find, a handy tool, but there are other possibilities.

National gun and hunting organizations such as the National Wild Turkey Federation, the National Rifle Association, the Ruffed Grouse Society, and conservation organizations such as the National Wildlife Federation and the Izaak Walton League all hold annual conventions that are attended by hunters. These conventions are usually rotated around the country and certainly there will be one reasonably close to your home. Join one or more of these organizations and join the cause or causes they are promoting—conservation of game, the protection of hunting rights, and the fight for gun ownership. The very fact that you are a member and working for the organization is a big step toward acceptance by fellow hunters. There is no better vehicle for working out highly satisfactory swap-hunt arrangements.

All such organizations have newsletters—or even magazines. Possibly you can put a notice in such a publication seeking a swap-a-hunt partner.

These are just some of the possibilities for locating some excellent hunting at a minimum of cost. Use your imagination and you may come up with other ways of making the necessary contact with a fellow hunter somewhere across the land.

Modern communication is making the world ever smaller. Fast mail service, FAX machines, and the telephone make modern communication fast and inexpensive. I haven't tried going on-line, though I do own a computer. I can see any number of possibilities for using this latest means of communication for contacting hunters out there who might like to swap a hunt with you.

Swapping hunts with fellow American across the land opens up endless possibilities for enjoying some good big game hunting on a budget.

Many easterners have excellent turkey hunting, the kind that produced this bird. If you do, maybe you can swap a turkey hunt for an antelope, elk, or mule deer hunt out west.

Chapter XII

Get Started Early

A few years ago a friend called me and said his very financially successful son wanted to take him on a Western big game hunt that fall. Did I have any ideas? Unfortunately I did, but not any that would help him. It was already late summer and they were hoping to get in a Western hunt that fall. My friend was a bird hunter, an avid one, and knew little about the mechanics of setting up a big game hunt. He was facing a couple of all but impossible problems.

A major one was that with, possibly a few exceptions, you cannot buy a Western big game license over the counter anymore. You have to apply early and usually enter a drawing for a limited number of permits. All of the deadlines had long since passed when my friend and his son began thinking about their big game hunt. Deadlines for applying for big game hunting licenses vary from state to state. The deadline for a Wyoming license as I write this is March 1, and consideration is being given to mov-

Successful antelope hunters have to apply for permits early. In many western states the deadline is as early as March 1 if you want to hunt that fall.

Hunts that produce elk like this are usually awarded on the basis of a lottery. Get your application in early if you want to stand a chance of being drawn.

ing it up to February 1. Arizona, on the other hand, has a May deadline. The deadlines in most Western big game states fall somewhere between those in these two popular states.

The terrific pressure from hunters around the world who desire to hunt the big Western states noted for their fine big game hunting no doubt has a lot to do with the deadlines and drawings from which a limited number of permits or licenses are issued. Not to do so would create crowded hunting conditions that would be not only dangerous, but could also make it almost impossible to enjoy a long-planned trip. I have no problem with this system. You just have to begin early enough in the year to stand a chance of getting a license or permit. A successful big game hunt today is a far cry from picking up the trusty old farm shotgun and wandering down the lane for a fat cottontail for dinner.

There are numerous exceptions, of course, but generally they exist in other parts of the country. You can go to deer-rich Alabama and buy a license from just about any license agent. This is also true in North Carolina, South Carolina, Virginia, and a number of other Southern states that offer good deer and turkey hunting. The same is true throughout much of the country. Over the years I have bought big game licenses over the counter in Alabama, Alaska, Mississippi, Ohio, Ontario, Pennsylvania, Quebec, Texas, and possibly other states or provinces that do not come readily to mind. Alaska, and perhaps some of the others, have since gone to lotteries. On the other hand I have had to enter drawings for permits in Arizona, Colorado, Idaho, New Mexico, the Northwest Territories, Wyoming, and other states.

In addition to the problem of filing deadlines for licenses or permits, there is the problem of finding an opening with a hunting guide or outfitter. These people book their hunts early, many at hunting shows across the country in January and February. Even if they have a couple of open dates, they may be ones that do not fit your schedule. You might end up having to juggle your scheduled vacation time, or even worse, having to postpone your hunt to another year. Eastern or Southern states may not have filing deadlines, but the guides and outfitters in those states can accommodate a limited number of hunters. For planning reasons they like to fill their slate as early as possible. Waiting too long might mean you will have to take your chances on running your own hunt on public land—which could be productive. But my friend and his son didn't have that in mind.

These were the kinds of problems my friend faced when he and his son made a last minute decision to go west and hunt big game. As I recall they decided not to make the effort, and I'm not sure that they ever took that hunt together. If they did, I didn't hear about it.

So you have to start early. But just how early is early enough? Ideally, your planning should begin as early as a full year before your planned hunt. This probably means September or October of the calendar year preceding the hunt. Many big game hunters return from fall trips and almost immediately begin working on one for the following fall. At the latest you should begin working on a fall hunt in early January of the year of the planned hunt. It's usually January before the latest hunting regulations are available.

First, you have to decide what kind of game you want to hunt and where you would like to hunt it. Chapter XVII, the final chapter of this book, gives a state-by-state listing of huntable big game. This is just a beginning, but it does narrow down your research—often to a half-dozen states. So you have a starting point. Watch outdoor magazines for features on the big game you plan to hunt. Look for hunting forecasts. Some are state by state, but others are regional. Call several of those states listed in Chapter XVII and ask to talk to one of their authorities on the animal you plan to hunt. After you have talked to several of them a pattern will probably begin to develop. Talk to friends and other big game hunters and get their ideas. Experienced big game hunters have on the tips of their tongues the best regions for most big game animals. Your local state wildlife agency will have some ideas even though the particular game does not live in your home state.

The earlier you develop this kind of information the better. Hence the reason for an early beginning.

With a state or province settled on you are now ready to move quickly toward firming up plans for an autumn dream hunt, maybe even the hunt of a lifetime. But you have one more move to make before keying in on licenses, permits, and a guide if you plan to use one. Get from the state game agency a breakdown of the harvest from the latest season. This will help you settle on a specific area. This was discussed in more detail in Chapter VII "Running Your Own Hunt."

With a specific area settled on, you are ready to begin nailing down a hunt for the fall. It doesn't matter whether you will run your own hunt or choose to engage a guide or outfitter. Most wildlife agencies break the state or province down into hunting areas depending mostly upon the needs of the resource. You will need the number of that hunting area before you engage a guide or outfitter, approach a landowner for a permit, or apply for a license and hunting permit. The quicker you can do this the more likely it is that you will get the area of your choice. Many guides, or landowners who allow hunting for a fee, won't even talk to you unless you have a license and permit for their area.

Even if you are not successful in drawing a license and permit for the region of your choice, you might be offered another area. Again move quickly. Other hunters will probably be in the same situation and they too will be on the telephone trying to locate hunting land or guides and outfitters. This happened to me several years ago on a Wyoming hunt. I applied for a mule deer license and permit for a hunting area I thought looked good. Apparently, I made a good choice because the limited number of permits went quickly and I was rejected. I was referred to

If you want to stand a chance at an elk such as these hunters have bagged, begin planning for next fall's hunt immediately upon returning from your current one.

another region, however, and immediately refiled. This time I was successful, quickly found a rancher who would let me hunt for a modest fee, and my hunt produced a good buck.

Once you get that particular hunting area located you are ready to address more specific details that will make your hunt run more smoothly and go down in your memory as one of the best. If you plan to stay in a motel make reservations immediately, even though your hunt is months away. At the peak of the season in states such as Colorado, Montana, or Wyoming it is almost impossible to get motel accommodations unless you have reservations. Call the chamber of commerce in the city in which you plan to stay and ask for recommendations. I personally like to check with the major motel chains and ask if they have a motel in the city or town I plan to use as a hunting base. The major chains have 800 numbers in your local telephone directory. You might even call the local motel of a major chain. They too can quickly tell you whether their chain has a unit available in the city you are considering. If they do they can give you the telephone number or even make the reservation for you. People who travel a lot keep motel directories of the major chains such as Days Inn or Holiday Inn.

If you plan to camp, the urgency to make reservations is usually not as critical. Will the rancher let you camp on his land? Settle this when you make reservations to hunt. If you want to go the commercial campground route get a campground directory from the tourism agency in the state where you will hunt. The wise thing to do is make a reservation early. Even campgrounds can fill at the peak of hunting seasons. You can get the tourism telephone number from the state wildlife agency when you talk to them about licenses and regulations.

If you plan to sign up with a professional guide or outfitter, someone who devotes full time to guiding, you won't have to worry about entering the lobby for a license and permit. The guide will do that for you. That is, of course, providing you sign up with him well in advance of the deadline for filing. So we come back to the golden rule, start planning for a big game hunt early. The better guiding services fill up early. Many of them have regular clients who book with them year after year. If you are a first timer, it behooves you to contact the guiding service early—the earlier the better. Some may even be booked full when you contact them and by then are accepting bookings for the following season.

If you are booking with a guiding service for the first time, there is still another reason to begin early. If you don't know the people, you should ask for references, hunters who have booked with them before. A professional guide or outfitter won't object to this. If you detect some hesitancy, let that be a signal to put up your guard. Check carefully any references you are given. This is not intended as a warning not to book with some ambitious young guide. After all, everyone has to start somewhere, and enterprising young people should be encouraged. If you get a young guide working his first season, his enthusiasm is likely going to offset any mistakes he makes. But back to those references. You must begin early enough to allow this process to work—getting the references from the guiding service and then contacting them before you book.

Most professional guiding services are going to take care of your living requirements providing shelter and food on your hunt, so you have no need to concern yourself about reserving space in motels or campgrounds.

Start early. With all of the loose ends tied down well in advance, you will enjoy even more the anticipation that builds as spring turns to summer and summer to fall, the season most likely to produce that big game hunt you have been dreaming of since you killed your first white-tailed deer.

The unheated body of a 4x4 pickup truck is ideal for getting meat and trophies across country.

Chapter XIII

Getting Meat and Trophies Home

Getting the meat and trophies home upon the completion of a successful big game hunt requires as much forethought or planning as does the transportation of the hunter. In fact it can sometimes be more difficult. Trophies can be less of a problem than the meat, though both call for planning in advance.

Down a deer in your home county and you have no problem. You know how to field dress the animal, and you have hunting companions nearby to help you drag it to your truck. Once there it can be as simple as driving to the nearest meat processing plant where you turn the job over to a professional to butcher, package, label, and freeze the meat. Later at your leisure you pick up your meat and drop it in your home freezer. If you are saving the antlers, head, or hide you simply pick them up after your meat processor has done his job and take them to your nearby taxidermist.

Simple enough. You have been through the process so many times it has become automatic.

But suppose you kill your animal, bear, elk, moose, or whatever, thousands of miles from home and your plane ticket is your transportation home. What now? You can treat the antlers as extra baggage and take them with you, but the meat or even a bear skin or head may require special attention.

If you are hunting with a guide he will probably take care of field dressing your animal, skinning it, and quartering it. He will also transport it to a local meat processing plant or to a point of shipment home. He may also package the meat for shipment. If you don't have a guide, you will have to take care of these tasks on your own. Hopefully, you have hunting partners to help you.

If you are flying, air freight is about the only option you have in shipping the meat, and you will be governed by the airline regulations in packaging it. Ideally you should turn it over to a local meat processor for butchering, labeling, and packing for the trip home by plane. This is the simplest approach. The airline will assume the responsibility of keeping the meat cool and it will arrive home in good condition. In the absence of a local meat processor, preparing it for shipment will become your responsibility—or your guide's if you have one. That being the case you should quarter the animal and pack it for shipping. Check with the airline before you leave home to find out how it should be packed. You will probably end up wrapping the meat in cheesecloth and packing it in cardboard boxes. Hopefully a local grocery store near the site of your hunt can supply you with the boxes. But before you leave home ask your airline about the availability of shipping cartons.

I've used air freight several times, and always with satisfactory results. The first time was on a Newfoundland moose hunt. It was a guided hunt and my guide and outfitter took care of the meat for me. It arrived home a couple of days after my return, but was not shipped to my home airport. I had to drive 50 miles to pick it up, but the airline had done an excellent job of taking care of the meat.

Years later I hunted musk-ox in the Northwest Territories early one November when the temperatures ranged around the 50 degrees below zero mark. Obviously, keeping the meat cool at the site of the hunt was no problem. The native guides kept most of the meat for their own use, but allowed their hunters to take home 50 pounds. As I recall, they packed the meat in a duffel bag and I checked it through to my Virginia home as extra baggage. It's cold even in Virginia in November so keeping the meat cool was no problem. I must admit, however, that the moose meat was much more tasty than that of the musk-ox . The difference, however, was in the animals—not how it was

The head of this bighorn sheep will make a handsome trophy if you get it to your taxidermist in good shape.

handled. In both cases the airlines took good care of the meat.

If you are taking a small amount of meat home, you can have it processed and frozen hard at the site of your hunt and check it through as extra baggage. Even a sturdy cardboard box will suffice for transporting it. Usually the cargo compartment of an airliner is cool and the frozen meat will remain so for a minimum of 24 hours. On most trips you will be home before the 24 hours elapse.

These big Texas white-tailed deer will make good venison if you get the meat home in good condition.

While air freight is an option, whether or not you travel by air, there are better and less costly choices when the hunter travels by automobile.

On numerous Western hunts I have had animals quartered on the site of the kill and hauled the meat home across the country in the back of my pickup truck. Usually the weather is cool enough during the hunting seasons to make this possible. One November my son-in-law and I bagged a couple of elk in Arizona, quartered them, and packed them in the body of my pickup truck. It was cool when we headed east on Interstate 40 out of Arizona, but the weather warmed considerably as we traveled east and we began to worry about our meat. To protect the meat we turned north in New Mexico and drove through the night to pick up Interstate 70 in St. Louis. Our decision got us into colder weather than we had anticipated, and we drove through a snowstorm from St. Louis to Virginia. It was worth it, though, as our quartered elk were frozen solid when we reached home.

When transporting quartered meat by automobile, you want to make sure it is stored so air can circulate between the quarters. I learned this when I was preparing to head for home on a Colorado elk hunt. I had field dressed the animal, and possibly could have carried it in that form, but on the suggestion of a fellow hunter I took it to a local meat processor and asked for his help. He unloaded the animal from my truck and told me it would be about an hour before he could get it ready to go. I roamed around the little Western town and picked up some gifts for my family. When I returned to the processor, the meat was ready. He loaded it for me and spaced it so air could circulate. "The meat is still warm," he warned me. "When you stop for the night make sure it is still spaced for air circulation." I checked into a motel that night, shuffled the meat around a bit and turned in comforted by the fact that it was being properly cared for. On that trip I was traveling alone across the country so hesitated to make the long trip home without someone to switch off the driving with. I did, however, get up early the next morning well rested and cleaned up from a long week of hunting with no shaving or showering. Rested and refreshed by a shave and a shower, I made it home stopping only for meals and to gas up. I knew that the quicker I got there the better off the meat would be.

I've used that approach several times to get meat home from a distant big game hunt. One thing I avoid, however, is hauling the meat where it is exposed to smells from the highway, the stench of diesel fuel, for example, or from oil burning wrecks that often travel even our best highways. Being exposed to the air usually also means being exposed to the direct rays of the sun and debris that is kicked into the air by vehicles just ahead. Just notice what your windshield collects on long trips and you will understand why you don't want to expose your meat to the same thing.

One thing to avoid is hauling your animal on the top of your vehicle. I see this often going and returning from Western trips. I'll admit that the sight of a couple of hunters headed home with their animals field dressed and carried visibly on the roof of their 4x4 vehicle thrills me, but it's not the best way to treat meat. If you insist on going this route, by all means leave the skin on the animal. It gives the meat some protection from highway debris and smells.

Modern automobiles don't have fenders that will permit it, but I was once driving west out of Washington, D.C. through Virginia and met a successful hunter with a bear resting on one front fender and a deer on the other. I assume he was returning from a successful hunt in West Virginia, but his meat, in addition to being exposed to highway pollution as described above, was exposed to the heat from his automobile engine.

Ideally, I like to handle my animals by field dressing them on the spot and taking them immediately to a nearby meat processor to cool, butcher, wrap, label, and possibly freeze the meat and hold if for me until I am ready to start home. This way you get home with your meat and drop it in your home freezer for use as you desire.

The only problem with this approach is how quickly the meat processor can get your meat ready for your return trip. The first time I used this approach was on a Wyoming

An ATV can be handy in getting game out of back country.

antelope hunt. A friend and I, on a low-budget hunt, both got our animals the first morning out. We field dressed the animals and took them to a processor in nearby Buffalo. In this case we were in no particular hurry to leave so we stayed in camp to fish for trout and hunt rabbits for a couple of days. By then the meat was ready to pick up. We dropped it into ice chests we had brought along for that purpose and got the meat home in excellent condition. The meat wasn't frozen solid, but it was thoroughly chilled, and since we drove straight through on the return trip also, we had it in our home freezers 36 hours later—along with some rabbits and rainbow trout.

If the weather is warm and you are concerned about meat carried home in an ice chest buy some dry ice. A small package in the top of an ice chest will keep the meat cold for several days—and it can be replaced if necessary. I've done this a couple of times on deer hunting trips to Texas, often warm country where even frozen meat requires more attention. Dry ice is sometimes hard to find. Look for it when you pass through major cities. On those Texas deer hunting trips my wife and I stopped several times en route home and replenished our dry ice. We were traveling in a station wagon both times and had to keep the meat inside where the vehicle was heated for our comfort.

A pickup truck is better for hauling meat because you can keep it in the unheated body of the vehicle. My 4x4 pickup truck has a protected body so the meat is not exposed to the rain and sun. In the absence of a covered body by all means protect the meat with a tarp or some other waterproof cover. Having a downpour soak the meat is worse than exposing it to the sun.

Smaller animals such as deer can be quartered and packed with ice in a large ice chest. Keep ice on the meat and it will turn out fine, particularly on short trips. One hot August I even brought a quartered deer home from South Carolina packed with ice in a chest. It was just a day's drive and I didn't have to replenish the ice. I hasten to add that the South Carolina deer season opens the middle of August so my kill was legal!

On still another trip some friends and I simply field dressed our animals and propped the cavities open so air would circulate through them, and hauled them home in the protected, but unheated, body of a pickup truck. There were six of us on that trip so we had no trouble driving straight through alternating at the driving. Those animals were in perfect condition when we reached home.

Tasty big game meat is one of the many rewards of a successful hunt. You don't have to look for "fat free" labels. That's a given that adds to your health as much as those days or weeks in a clean outdoor environment where such game animals thrive. Take care of your meat and it will help take care of you.

Chapter XIV

Care of Equipment

Purchase the best hunting equipment you can afford, take care of it, and it will last for years. Some gear such as guns and knives can last through several generations. Even clothing, when properly cared for, can last for years. I have a red plaid hunting jacket that I bought from L. L. Bean over 30 years ago. I don't wear it as much as I used to because blaze orange as a safety precaution has long since replaced red, the original safety hunting color. But I still get a lot of wear out of that comfortable old jacket, even though the cuffs are slightly worn. If they get worse, however, a good seamstress can repair them.

Hunters as a group can be hard on their clothing and equipment. There are exceptions, of course. Some clean the bluing off their guns. They do too good a job. At the other extreme there are those who neglect their equipment shamefully. The guns they pass on to the next generation are going to have pitted bores and badly neglected working parts. Reasonable care, mixed in with good old common sense, will allow you to get a full measure of use out of your equipment. It needs attention throughout a hunt as well as at the conclusion. Care in the course of a hunt is equally as important as the cleaning that follows the hunt.

Hunting by its very nature is hard on equipment. The weather is a major factor—rain, sleet, snow, wind, an unrelenting sun, and temperatures that can range from well below freezing to over a hundred degrees and heat waves dancing before your eyes. Fortunately, most hunting is done in more moderate weather. Of the various conditions the weather can toss at you, rain is probably the worst, a steady drizzle that slowly seeps through your clothing and equipment or a downpour that does the same

You don't want your equipment to fail when you come head to head with a wild boar.

more quickly. Protecting yourself and your equipment from the elements is a basic precaution. Blowing sand is also difficult to deal with and tough on firearms and other equipment with moving parts. A little advance study to determine what kind of weather you are going to encounter will go a long ways toward protecting your equipment. You can plan for the worst.

Transportation can also be tough on equipment. Having a rifle bounce around in the body of a pickup truck, in an unprotected open boat, on a bushplane, or on an ATV can knock the sights out of alignment and even do more extensive damage. The same is true for compound bows, blackpowder rifles, and shotguns. The best protection in transit is a good case, one that will absorb the shocks and catch flying debris. I recall handing my 30/06 rifle to an Alaskan bush pilot, assuming he would store it safely on a fly-in trip for some back country bear hunting. My first shot, an easy one at less than 50 yards, was a clean miss. I couldn't believe it until I got back to the cabin and bore sighted my rifle. It was way off, causing me to miss badly on a golden opportunity. Fortunately, I was able to sight it in again and continue the hunt, my old confidence in my pet rifle restored.

Your rifle, conventional or blackpowder, and your bow and arrows are a major concern on hunting trips. If they malfunction because of neglect, your trip will be a complete bust. The hunt of your lifetime might even be spoiled. One precaution is a backup, but I've been in deep wilderness areas with hunters who carried only one rifle. On a pack trip where weight is a consideration, an additional rifle can be a handicap. A session at a benchrest prior to the hunt to make sure your rifle is sighted in correctly and functioning properly is a must. Run a patch through the bore when you are finished and it should be ready to go.

En route, the firearm should be carried in a case, a hard one or one that is padded. Such a case offers a lot of protection irrespective of the mode of transportation. There are places where a case is impractical, on a pack trip, for example, where rifles are carried in saddle scabbards.

In the course of a hunt, awareness that your rifle is vulnerable will prompt you to give it tender loving care. When you pause to take a rest, do some glassing, eat lunch, or for some other reason, give consideration to where you place your rifle. Don't drop it in wet grass, snow, or in sand or mud.

When fighting your way through a thicket or wading a swamp be sure you rifle is protected from blows that might knock the sights out of alignment or do other damage, and attempt to protect it from splashing water or mud.

A rifle often gets neglected after a successful kill. In the joy of the moment the hunter's prize consumes all of his attention. Temper all of that enthusiasm just enough to allow concern for the rifle that did its job for you. Don't throw it aside to be neglected completely while your attention focuses on your game and getting it back to your vehicle, camp, cabin, or home.

The rifle or bow needs particular attention when hunting from an elevated stand. Instead of climbing to the stand with the rifle or bow slung over you shoulder, attach a strong cord or line to the bow or rifle and make your climb with the other end in your hand. Once in place, carefully pull the bow or rifle up. Avoid letting it swing against the stand or tree as you do so. Using the line to pull

This successful Newfoundland moose hunter was ready and so was his rifle and other equipment when he got his opportunity.

the bow or rifle up eliminates the possibility of banging it against the stand as you climb—or even worse dropping it. When leaving the stand reverse the procedure.

Back in camp give the rifle or bow the same consideration you give yourself. Use a dry cloth or paper towel to wipe it down, removing drops of water, dust, or other foreign matter. If it has been subjected to rain or snow, break it down for attention. Equipment that has been thoroughly socked by rain, snow, or even accidentally dunked in a lake or stream should be dried as much as possible and then placed near the campfire or cabin stove to dry more thoroughly. That done it should then be oiled thoroughly.

Ammunition, knives, compasses, and other incidental gear generally fare better in the fields and woods or on the water than do rifles and archery equipment. That doesn't mean they should be neglected. Modern ammunition handles all kinds of weather amazingly well, but that doesn't mean it

Successful mule deer hunter with his well-cared-for rifle. One shot did the job for him.

should be neglected. "Keep your powder dry," is a phrase that was coined back in the days when both hunting and warfare were carried on with black powder. Get it wet and it wouldn't function. It's advice the modern black powder hunter has to adhere to. This means storing your black powder in water-proof containers. Firing caps also need to be kept dry.

Otherwise you are going to have to replace them—unnecessary expense.

Modern hunting knives are durable. They can take a lot of abuse. A fine cutting edge needs protection, however. Keep your knives in their sheaths when not in use. And keep them as dry as possible or some rust may occur. Hunting knives are called upon for all kinds of functions in addition to field dressing or quartering game. They tend to lose that edge, and it has to be honed frequently. A small whetting stone should be available to attend to this matter, otherwise the knife will soon become too dull to do its job. A good knife like a good rifle will survive several generations of hunters. More are lost than eventually worn out.

Compasses and watches are somewhat delicate instruments that can take a lot of abuse, but function better and last longer when given the proper care. Keep them dry and try to avoid hard impact with the likes of boulders, trees, and other unyielding objects encountered in most hunting grounds.

Hunting clothing is going to be subjected to rips and tears and wetting from weather as well as spray from boats, and the not unlikely possibility of being soaked in a lake or stream when a hunter makes a careless move. There isn't a lot you can do about clothing in the hunting grounds except to avoid as many of the inevitable rips or tears as possible. A simple sewing kit that takes up a minimum of room can prevent further damage to a rip or tear by making temporary repairs in the hunting grounds.

Wet clothing should be dried as quickly and as thoroughly as possible, and mud or ice and snow removed. Take advantage of a campfire or cabin stove to dry out your clothing.

There is no item of clothing more important than boots or shoes. Leather boots should be cleaned and oiled before a hunting trip and dried as frequently as possible in the hunting grounds. Wet leather boots or shoes should be dried slowly and then treated with a good boot or shoe preservative. Boots and shoes are not going to last as long as hunting jackets, caps and hats, or other equipment, but give them the best care you can, and they will last for years, keeping your feet dry and warm while hunting in all kinds of

This deer hunter and his rifle are ready should this downed deer suddenly leap up and try to escape. It happens occasionally, but if your rifle is in good shape it doesn't present a problem.

weather. The same is true of socks. Take along enough pairs to change daily and they will keep your feet in better shape and last longer. Wet socks should be dried as quickly as possible after they have been removed.

Regardless of how well you treat your guns and other hunting equipment in the field, it is storage at home between trips that truly prolongs their life.

Back from an extended hunting trip or at the end of a season, I clean my guns thoroughly, oil them, and store them in my gun chest away from dampness or heat. I check them periodically during the off season to make sure rust does not accumulate. Regardless of how well you store them, specks of rust sometimes occur during the long months between hunting seasons. I don't break my guns down to the point that I have trouble reassembling them. I'm not that good a gunsmith, but occasionally I take the ones I use most often to my local gunsmith who cleans them thoroughly for a modest fee. He gives particular attention to the bores of my rifles, primarily my 30/06 that does yeoman duty on big game and my pair of .22's that get a lot of use on small game. Despite my best efforts, slight buildup of fouling and cleaning oil begins to accumulate and the rifles lose some of their pinpoint accuracy. A professional gunsmith, he is able to restore those tight groups I seek.

Modern smokeless gunpowder is amazingly clean, and normally I don't give my guns a thorough cleaning until the end of the season. If they get wet or dirty, I simply wipe them dry with a clean cloth and add a little oil if it seems necessary. Rarely is it. I keep them stored in a clean and dry gun case.

Knives I clean and run through the dishwasher, give them a couple of strokes with a whetting stone, and store them where they will stay dry. One of my hunting knives is over 40 years old and in as good condition as it was when I bought it. So is its leather sheath—which I've never oiled. If I don't lose it, one of my heirs is going to inherit a good hunting knife.

Clothing should be cleaned or laundered as needed throughout a hunting season, particularly upon returning from a trip. Rips and tears should be repaired before they get worse. During the off season clothing should be stored only after cleaning or laundering. It will be all ready to go the next opening day. Boots and shoes should be thoroughly clean of mud, washed thoroughly and dried before storing. Leather ones should be oiled thoroughly. Clothing is rarely a lifetime investment, but properly taken care of, it will give good service for years.

There is no secret to saving on hunting equipment. You select quality products, shop wisely, and take good care of your investment in big game hunting. Do so and it will last you for years, making the minimum of a dent in your budget.

Chapter XV

A Look at Bowhunting and Blackpowder

Both bowhunting and blackpowder hunting are making major inroads into big game hunting today. Much of the attraction is the hunter's desire to recapture some of the rich history of hunting, to step for a moment into the shoes of the Indians and frontiersmen who contributed so much to the rich history of hunting in America. These hardy hunters of old knew their quarry intimately. Success demanded it. Their bows and old muskets were primitive by modern standards. Even so there were some legendary marksmen among those hunters of yesteryear, sharpshooters whose skills were much sought after during the wars, large and small, that helped shape our nation.

The archery equipment that we take into the fields and woods today is a product of modern technology though the principles are the same as those employed so successfully by the American Indians whose hunting techniques we attempt to emulate. We began with long bows much like those the Indians hunted and fought their battles with—and I suppose, like the legendary Robin Hood of Sherwood Forest. Modern technology eventually developed the recurve bow, and more recently that same modern technology produced the now popular compound bow. Bowhunting took a big step forward when the compound bow came on the scene. Today bowhunters are taking an increasingly larger portion of the total white-tailed deer harvest, and many successfully hunt all kinds of other big game.

Those taking up bowhunting for the first time would be well advised to choose a good compound bow, though experienced archers still fall back on their old recurves for

A successful Virginia bowhunter with a sika deer bull. The sika is actually a Far East member of the elk family, hence "bull" instead of "buck."

certain hunting situations. "It's faster," one veteran bowhunter told me.

Though many modern blackpowder hunters insist on staying with the muskets of frontier days, the old flintlocks, modern technology has again taken the old muzzle-loading principle and produced a modern in-line or percussion rifle that eliminates some of the old problems that the hunter faced with his beloved flintlock. "Keep your powder dry," is still meaningful advice, but less important to those hunting with modern percussion in-line rifles.

Most deer hunters shoot .50 caliber muzzle-loaders, but for elk and other larger game a .54 caliber or possibly .58 is the usual choice. Equipped with a telescopic scope, the modern in-line muzzle-loading rifle is an excellent hunting tool.

Modern bowhunting and blackpowder hunting are broad subjects that can be little more than touched upon in a book of this nature. Big game hunters who want to step into the past and revive some of the glories of the old days will find a wealth of helpful information out there in specialized books and hunting magazines.

A nice black bear taken with a musket muzzleloader.

Like the conventional rifle hunters, archery and blackpowder hunters should familiarize themselves with the hunting regulations of any state or province they plan to hunt. This is particularly true on self-guided hunts. Generally competent guides are familiar with the regulations in their own hunting area. There may be exceptions, but as a general rule both the bow and arrow and muzzle-loading rifles are legal during any conventional firearms season. There the primitive weapons fan hunts alongside the hunter bearing a conventional rifle. Instead of enjoying an advantage, he is at a disadvantage. This was the case before someone got the idea of special seasons for primitive weapons hunters.

That's the true advantage the modern archer or muzzle-loading hunter enjoys—special seasons. He usually gets the first crack at a new crop of game. In my home state of Virginia bowhunters are in the woods for bear, deer, and turkeys approximately six weeks before the conventional firearms season opens. Not only that, they are allowed either-sex deer hunting their entire season, and both hen turkeys and gobblers are fair game for them. Muzzle-loading hunters also get a special early season. They are in the fields and woods two weeks before the conventional firearms deer season opens. They also enjoy antlerless hunting throughout the season—and they hunt at the peak of the rut when trophy bucks are most vulnerable. In the western part of Virginia where the conventional firearms season is a two-week one that ends in early December, bowhunters and muzzle-loading hunters can continue to hunt into early January.

I mention Virginia as an example. Generally archers and primitive weapons fans enjoy this advantage in seasons throughout much of North America. Deer are the major big game affected by these special seasons, but in many states and provinces there are archery seasons for bear, boar, elk, and other game. There seems to be somewhat of a pattern of early seasons for bowhunters and late ones for muzzle-loaders. In a number of states the muzzle-loaders are allowed to hunt after the conventional firearms season closes but not before the conventional season.

Some of these seasons open very early. As I write this, California opens its deer archery season in early July.

One advantage the early archery seasons offer the big game hunter is the opportunity to get in some hunting during vacation time. It means that students who have several free months in the summer, but have difficulty getting away in the fall, can do some out-of-state big game hunting. And members of a family on the annual summer vacation can work in a couple of days of hunting. This may mean the father only, a father and son, or better still the entire family. Just as an example, a family, or members of a family, vacationing in Yellowstone National Park, could swing through Utah on the way home and enjoy several days of deer hunting. Currently the Utah archery deer season opens in the middle of July. Some research and planning will turn up a number of such possibilities where a family vacation can be stretched to include some bowhunting. It combines a hunting budget with a vacation budget resulting in a substantial savings in travel and other costs.

Hunters in the teaching profession at all levels, because they enjoy long summer vacations, have trouble getting away for even a week or two at the peak of fall big game hunting seasons. Bowhunting is one solution to this problem and muzzle-loading hunting is also to a lesser degree. Check the major hunting magazines. Several of them give annual summaries of hunting seasons across America. They can be valuable tools in the early planning stages, though when you get down to a specific state or province you need more detailed regulations from that particular state.

Bowhunting, particularly, gives the hunter a break on the weather. He generally hunts when the weather is mild, Indian Summer often, and even in the heat of the summer in some states. This means less of an investment in clothing. Cotton camouflage will usually meet his needs, and if the weather gets cooler he can wear it over long johns or a light sweater or vest. If he camps he does so in warm or moderate weather. His camping needs are lighter. He doesn't have to worry about a heated tent, for example, or

A nice white-tailed buck taken with an in-line muzzleloader.

other special needs for cold-weather camping. Even transportation into back country is less of a problem. He doesn't have to worry about frozen water if he goes by canoe, or snow-filled mountain gaps if he goes by ATV, 4x4, or pack horses. All in all it's a more pleasant and less expensive expedition.

One disadvantage of hunting during the warmer seasons is the need for special care for the meat. It should be field dressed immediately and the cavity propped open so it can cool. And the quicker it can be transported to a meat processor the better. Getting it home, particularly across country, also requires more attention. It should be iced down, preferably with dry ice.

Sometimes archery and muzzle-loading hunters get a break on license costs, but it is rare. In fact in most states the primitive weapons hunters are required to purchase an archery or muzzle-loading license in addition to the regular big game license. But look into the possibility of short-term licenses. They are available in a number of Southeastern states.

A bowhunter takes aim from a treestand.

A major advantage archery and muzzle-loading hunters enjoy is a special season during which they have the hunting grounds to themselves. An archer does not compete with firearms hunters, either blackpowder or conventional, and the blackpowder hunter does not compete with conventional firearms hunters or archers. Another advantage is a higher chance of drawing a permit if a lottery drawing is part of the process. While their numbers are growing, neither the archers nor muzzle-loaders approach the numbers of conventional firearms hunters out there. Consequently they do not face the competition for permits that conventional hunters do. No savings in cost there, but a higher chance of drawing a permit. In some instances bowhunters do not have to enter a lottery. They can buy their permits over the counter.

Cost-wise there is very little difference between a quality conventional bolt-action rifle and a bow or muzzle-load of equal quality. Shop and you might find the quality primitive weapons slightly less costly, but add sights, slings, and other accessories and the difference is small—but still worthy of consideration.

Bowhunting and blackpowder, like hunting big game with conventional firearms can be expensive, but the hunter who follows the suggestions outlined in this book can still enjoy these new approaches to hunting and stay within his budget.

Good hunting!

Chapter XVI

Listing of Names, Addresses, and Telephone Numbers of Various State and Provincial Game Agencies

The game agencies of the various states and provinces are good sources of information, the place to begin when planning an out-of-state hunt. At the minimum they can provide information on the status of game populations, public hunting lands, regulations, licenses, seasons, and game harvests. Many can also provide lists of guides and sometimes private land open to hunting for a fee. The addresses and telephone numbers given are the latest, but subject to change. If you experience a problem call information in the city indicated and ask for the current telephone number.

Alabama Department of Conservation and Natural
Resources: Division of Game and Fish
64 North Union Street, Room 728
Montgomery, AL 36130, telephone 334/242-3465

Alaska Department of Fish and Game
P.O. Box 25526
Juneau, AK 99802-5526, telephone 907/465-4100

Arizona Game and Fish Department
2221 West Greenway Road
Phoenix, AZ 85023-4312, telephone 602/789-3278
    Can furnish list of guides

Arkansas Game and Fish Commission
Number 2 Natural Resources Drive
Little Rock, AR 72205, telephone 501/223-6305
Can furnish list of corporate landowners who allow hunting

California Department of Fish and Game
1416 Ninth Street
P.O. Box 944209Sacramento, CA 94244-2090, telephone 916/653-7667
Can furnish list of guides and landowners who allow hunting

Colorado Department of Natural Resources
Division of Wildlife
6060 Broadway
Denver, CO 80216, telephone 303/291-7208
For guides call Colorado Outfitters Association 303/841-7760

Connecticut Bureau of Natural Resources
Department of Environmental Protection
79 Elm Street
Hartford, CT 06106-5127, telephone 203/566-4477

Delaware Department of Natural Resources and
Environmental Control
Division of Fish and Wildlife
P.O. Box 1401, 89 Kings Highway
Dover, DE 72205, telephone 302/739-5295

Florida Game and Fresh Water Fish Commission
620 South Meridian Street
Tallahassee, FL 32399-1600, telephone 904/488-2975

Georgia Department of Natural Resources
Wildlife Resources Division
2070 U.S. Highway 278 Southeast
Social Circle, GA 30279, telephone 770/918-6401

Hawaii Board of Land & Natural Resources
P.O. Box 621, 1151 Punchbowl Street
Honolulu, HI 96809, telephone 808/587-0400
Can furnish list of hunting guides

Idaho Department of Fish and Game
P.O. Box 25, 600 South Walnut Street
Boise, ID 83707, telephone 208/334-5159
Can furnish list of hunting guides

Illinois Department of Natural Resources
Division of Wildlife Resources
Lincoln Tower Plaza
524 South Second Street
Springfield, IL 62701-1787, telephone 217/785-0075

Indiana Department of Natural Resources
Division of Fish and Wildlife
402 West Washington Street, Room W-273
Indianapolis, IN 46204, telephone 317/232-4080

Iowa Department of Natural Resources
Wallace State Office Building
East 9th and Grand Avenue
Des Moines, IA 50319-0034, telephone 515/281-5385

Kansas Department of Wildlife and Parks
900 Southwest Jackson Street, Room 502
Topeka, KS 66612-1223, telephone 913/296-2281
Can furnish list of hunting guides

Kentucky Department of Fish and Wildlife Resources
One Game Farm Road
Frankfort, KY 40601, telephone 502/564-3400
Can furnish list of hunting guides

Louisiana Department of Wildlife and Fisheries
P.O. Box 98000
Baton Rouge, LA 70898-9000, telephone 504/765-2623

Maine Department of Inland Fisheries and Wildlife
284 State House Road, Station #21
Augusta, ME 04333-0021, telephone 207/287-5202
Can furnish list of hunting guides

Maryland Department of Natural Resources
Tawes State Office Building B-2
580 Taylor Avenue
Annapolis, MD 21401, telephone 410/974-3195

Massachusetts Division of Fisheries and Wildlife
State Office building
100 Cambridge Street, Room 1902
Boston, MA 02202, telephone 617/727-3155

Michigan Department of Natural Resources
Stevens T. Mason Building
P.O. Box 30028
Lansing, MI 48909-7528, telephone 517/373-2329

Minnesota Department of Natural Resources
Division of Fish and Wildlife
Box 7 DNR Building
500 Lafayette Road
St. Paul, MN 55155-4020, telephone 612/297-1308
 Can furnish list of landowners who permit hunting

Mississippi Department of Wildlife Conservation
P.O. Box 451
2350 Highway 80 West at Ellis Avenue
Jackson, MS 39205-0451, telephone 601/364-2000
 Can refer hunters to foundation that maintains list of
landowners who allow hunting

Missouri Department of Conservation
P.O. Box 180, 2901 West Truman Blvd.
Jefferson City, MO 65102-0180, telephone 573/751-4115

Montana Department of Fish, Wildlife and Parks
1420 East Sixth Avenue
Helena, MT 59620, telephone 406/444-3186

Nebraska Game and Parks Commission
P.O. Box 30370, 2200 North 33rd Street
Lincoln, NE 68503-0370, telephone 402/471-5539

Nevada Department of Wildlife
P.O. Box 10678, 1100 Valley Road
Reno, NV 89520-0022, telephone 702/688-1599
 Can furnish list of guides and landowners who allow
hunting

New Hampshire Fish and Game Department
2 Hazen Drive
Concord, NH 03301, telephone 603/271-3422
 Can furnish list of hunting guides

New Jersey Department of Environmental Protection
Division of Fish, Game, and Wildlife
CN400
Trenton, NJ 08625, telephone 609/292-9410
 Can furnish partial list of landowners who allow hunting

New Mexico Department of Game and Fish
P.O. Box 25112
Santa Fe, NM 87504-5112, telephone 505/827-7899
 Can furnish list of hunting guides and landowners who
allow hunting for antelope and elk

New York Department of Environmental Conservation
Division of Fish and Wildlife
50 Wolf Road, Room 524
Albany, NY 12233-4750, telephone 518/457-5690

North Carolina Wildlife Resources Commission
Archdale Building
512 North Salisbury Street
Raleigh, NC 27604-1188, telephone 919/733-3391

North Dakota Game and Fish Department
100 North Bismarck Expressway
Bismarck, ND 58501-5095, telephone 701/328-6300
 Can furnish list of hunting guides

Ohio Department of Natural Resources
Division of Wildlife
1840 Belcher Drive, Building G-1
Columbus, OH 43224-1329, telephone 614/265-6300

Oklahoma Department of Wildlife Conservation
P.O. Box 53465, 1801 North Lincoln Drive
Oklahoma City, OK 73152, telephone 405/521-3851

Oregon Department of Fish and Wildlife
P.O. Box 59, 5201 Southwest First Avenue
Portland, OR 97207, telephone 503/872-5310
    Can furnish list of hunting guides

Pennsylvania Game Commission
2001 Elmerton Avenue
Harrisburg, PA 17110-9797, telephone 717/787-4250

Rhode Island Division of Fish and Wildlife
Oliver Stedman Government Center
4808 Tower Hill Road
Wakefield, RI 02879, telephone 401/277-3075

South Carolina Wildlife and Marine Resources Department
P.O. Box 167, 1000 Assembly Street
Columbia, SC 29202, telephone 803/734-4007

South Dakota Department of Game, Fish, and Parks
523 East Capitol
Pierre, SD 57501-3182, telephone 605/773-3387
    Can help to a degree with information on guides and
landowners who allow hunting

Tennessee Wildlife Resources Agency
Ellington Agricultural Center
P.O. Box 40747-Edmondson Pike
Nashville, TN 37204, telephone 615/781-6552

Texas Parks and Wildlife Department
4200 Smith School Road
Austin, TX 78744, telephone 512/389-4802
    Contact Texas Wildlife Association 1-800/460-5494 for list
of guides and private leases

Utah Division of Wildlife Resources
1596 West North Temple
Salt Lake City, UT 84116-3195 telephone 801/538-4703

Vermont Department of Fish and Wildlife
Waterbury Complex, 10 South
103 South Main Street
Waterbury, VT 05676, telephone 802/241-3730
Can furnish a list of hunting guides

Virginia Department of Game and Inland Fisheries
P.O. Box 11104, 4010 West Broad Street
Richmond, VA 23230-1104, telephone 804/367-1000
Can furnish list of corporate landowners who allow
hunting

Washington Department of Fish and Wildlife
600 Capitol Way, North
Olympia, WA 98501-1091, telephone 360/902-2225
No formal listing of landowners who allow hunting, but
can make suggestions

West Virginia Department of Natural Resources
Division of Wildlife Resources
1900 Kanawha Boulevard East
Charleston, WV 25303, telephone 304/558-2771
Can furnish list of hunting guides and corporate
landowners who allow hunting

Wisconsin Department of Natural Resources
P.O. Box 7921, 101 South Webster Street
Madison, WI 53707, telephone 608/266-2121
Can furnish list of hunting guides

Wyoming Game and Fish Department
5400 Bishop Boulevard
Cheyenne, WY 82006, telephone 307/777-4600
Can furnish list of some landowners who permit hunting,
and for list of guides contact Wyoming State Board of
Outfitters and Professional Guides, 1750 Wertland Road, Suite
166, Cheyenne, WY 82002, telephone 307/777-5323

Alberta Environmental Protection
Fish and Wildlife Services
9945 108th Street
Edmonton, Alberta, Canada TSK 2G6, telephone 403/427-6729

British Columbia Ministry of Environment, Lands, and Parks
Wildlife Branch
780 Blenshard Street
Victoria, British Columbia, Canada V8V 1X4, telephone 604/
387-9717

Manitoba Department of Natural Resources
1495 St. James Street, Box 22
Winnipeg, Manitoba, Canada R3H 0W9, telephone 204/945-
6784

New Brunswick Department of Natural Resources and Energy
Fish and Wildlife Branch
P.O. Box 6000
Fredericton, New Brunswick, Canada E3B 5H1, telephone 560/
453-2440

Newfoundland and Labrador Department of Natural Resources
Wildlife Division
P.O. Box 8700
St. Johns, Newfoundland, Canada A1B 4J6, telephone 709/729-
2815

Northwest Territories Department of Renewable Resources
Government of the Northwest Territories
600, 5102-50 Avenue
Yellowknife, Northwest Territories, Canada X1A 3S8, telephone
403/920-8716

Nova Scotia Department of Natural Resources
P.O. Box 698
Halifax, Nova Scotia, Canada B3J 2T9, telephone 902/424-4297

Ontario Ministry of Natural Resources
900 Bay Street, Room MI-73
Macdonald Block
Toronto, Ontario, Canada M7A 2C1, telephone 416/314-2000

Prince Edward Island Fish and Wildlife Division
Department of Environmental Resources
P.O. Box 2000
Charlottetown, Prince Edward Island, Canada C1A 7N8,
telephone 902/368-4683

Quebec Ministry of the Environment
Fish and Wildlife Division
Adisige Maric Guyart
150 Boulevard Street, Cyrelle East
Quebec City, Quebec, Canada G1R 5V7, telephone 418/643-2207

Saskatchewan Environment and Resource Management
3211 Albert Street
Regina, Saskatchewan, Canada S4S 5W6, telephone 306/787-9034

Yukon Territory Department of Renewable Resources
P.O. Box 2703
Whitehorse, Yukon Territory, Canada Y1A 2C6, telephone 403/667-5221

Chapter XVII

State and Provincial Listing of Big Game Species

Hunters planning an out-of-state big game hunt first have to know the general range of the game they are interested in. To that end we are listing below the big game species found in each of the 50 states and 11 Canadian provinces. Of the 61 jurisdictions only Canada's Prince Edward Island doesn't offer big game hunting. Deer are the most prevalent, but all of the 50 states and several of the Canadian provinces offer wild turkey hunting. Some wildlife managers may question classifying the wild turkey as big game, but it is so classified in many states and is included here. The coyote is rarely considered as big game, but it is an elusive animal, difficult to hunt, and its numbers are growing dramatically all across North America. In a few isolated cases a specific species is available only to residents of the state or province.

With that background let's take a look at what the various states and provinces have for the big game hunter. Listed are huntable populations only. Alaska, for example, has a population of polar bears, but they are not hunted.

Alabama:	White-tail deer, wild hog, and wild turkey
Alaska:	Bison, black bear, brown or grizzly bear, caribou, elk, moose, mountain goat, muskoxen, sheep, Sitka deer, and wolf
Arizona:	Antelope, bison, black bear, Coues deer, coyote, elk, javelina, mountain lion, mule deer, sheep, white-tail deer
Arkansas:	Black bear, coyote, white-tail deer, wild boar, and wild turkey

California:	Antelope, black bear, blacktail deer, coyote, mule deer, elk, sheep, wild pigs, and wild turkey
Colorado:	Antelope, black bear, coyote, elk, moose, mountain goat, mountain lion, mule deer, sheep, white-tail deer, and wild turkey
Connecticut:	Coyote, white-tail deer, and wild turkey
Delaware:	White-tail deer and wild turkey
Florida:	White-tail deer, wild hogs, and wild turkey
Georgia:	Black bear, coyote, white-tail deer, wild hogs, and wild turkey
Hawaii:	Axis deer, blacktail deer, feral goat, feral sheep, mouflon sheep, wild pigs, and wild turkey
Idaho:	Antelope, black bear, coyote, elk, moose, mountain goat, mountain lion, mule deer, sheep, white-tail deer, and wild turkey
Illinois:	Coyote, white-tail deer, and wild turkey
Indiana:	White-tail deer and wild turkey
Iowa:	Coyote, white-tail deer, and wild turkey
Kansas:	Antelope, mule deer, white-tail deer, and wild turkey
Kentucky:	Coyote, white-tail deer, wild boar, and wild turkey
Louisiana:	Coyote, white-tail deer, wild hog, and wild turkey
Maine:	Black bear, coyote, moose, white-tail deer, and wild turkey
Maryland:	Coyote, Sitka deer, white-tail deer, and wild turkey
Massachusetts:	Black bear, coyote, white-tail deer, and wild turkey
Michigan:	Black bear, elk, white-tail deer, and wild turkey

Minnesota:	Black bear, moose, white-tail deer, and wild turkey
Mississippi:	White-tail deer, wild hogs, and wild turkey
Missouri:	Coyote, white-tail deer, and wild turkey
Montana:	Antelope, black bear, elk, mountain goat, mountain lion, moose, mule deer, sheep, white-tail deer, and wild turkey
Nebraska:	Antelope, coyote, elk, mule deer, white-tail deer, and wild turkey
Nevada:	Antelope, coyote, elk, mountain goat, mountain lion, mule deer, sheep, and wild turkey
New Hampshire:	Black bear, coyote, moose, white-tail deer, and wild turkey
New Jersey:	Coyote, white-tail deer, and wild turkey
New Mexico:	Antelope, aoudad, Barbary sheep, black bear, Coues deer, coyote, elk, ibex, javelina, mountain lion, mule deer, oryx, sheep, white-tail deer, and wild turkey
New York:	Black bear, coyote, white-tail deer, and wild turkey
North Carolina:	Black bear, white-tail deer, wild boar, and wild turkey.
North Dakota:	Antelope, elk, coyote, moose, mule deer, sheep, white-tail deer, and wild turkey
Ohio:	White-tail deer, wild boar, and wild turkey
Oklahoma:	Antelope, coyote, white-tail deer, wild hog, and wild turkey
Oregon:	Antelope, black bear, blacktail deer, coyote, elk, mountain goat, mountain lion, sheep, white-tail deer, and wild turkey
Pennsylvania:	Black bear, coyote, white-tail deer, and wild turkey

Rhode Island:	White-tail deer and wild turkey
South Carolina:	Black bear, coyote, white-tail deer, wild hogs, and wild turkey
South Dakota:	Antelope, bison, coyote, elk, mountain goat, sheep, white-tail deer, and wild turkey
Tennessee:	Black bear, white-tail deer, wild boar, and wild turkey
Texas:	Antelope, aoudad, javelina, mule deer, white-tail deer, wild hog, and wild turkey
Utah:	Antelope, bison, elk, moose, mountain goat, mule deer; sheep, and wild turkey
Vermont:	Black bear, coyote, moose, white-tail deer, and wild turkey
Virginia:	Black bear, coyote, sika deer, white-tail deer, wild hog, and wild turkey
Washinton:	Black bear, blacktail deer, coyote, moose, mountain goat, mountain lion, mule deer, sheep, white-tail deer, and wild turkey
West Virginia:	Black bear, white-tail deer, wild boar, and wild turkey
Wisconsin:	Black bear, coyote, white-tail deer, and wild turkey
Wyoming:	Antelope, black bear, elk, coyote, moose, mountain goat, mountain lion, mule deer, sheep, white-tail deer, and wild turkey
Alberta:	Black bear, elk, mountain lion, moose, mule deer, sheep, and white-tail deer
British Columbia:	Black bear, blacktail deer, elk, grizzly bear, moose, mountain goat, mountain lion, mule deer, sheep, white-tail deer, and wolf
Manitoba:	Black bear, elk, caribou, moose, mule deer, white-tail deer, and wolf

New Brunswick:	Black bear, coyote, moose, and white-tail deer
Newfoundland &Labrador:	Black bear, coyote, caribou, and moose
Northwest Territories:	Black bear, caribou, grizzly bear, moose, mountain goat, musk-ox, polar bear, sheep, and wolf
Nova Scotia:	Black bear, coyote, moose, and white-tail deer
Ontario	Black bear, moose, coyote, white-tail deer, wild turkey, and wolf
Prince Edward Island:	No big game
Quebec:	Black bear, caribou, coyote, moose, white-tail deer, wild turkey, and wolf
Saskatchewan:	Antelope, black bear, caribou, coyote, elk, moose, mule deer, and white-tail deer
Yukon Territory:	Black bear, caribou, coyote, grizzly bear, moose, mountain goat, sheep, and wolf

Convenient Order Form
I would like to have additional copies of this book.
Big Game Hunting on a Budget

Please mail _____ copies to the address below:

Name_____

Address_____

_____

Enclosed please find check or money order in the amount of $9.95 that includes postage and handling for each book.

Please mail to: W. Horace Carter
                         Atlantic Publishing Company
                                 P.O. Box 67
                            Tabor City, NC 28463
                            Phone 919-653-3153
                    VISA and MasterCard Orders Accepted.
                  (Tear out and mail this sheet to publisher.)

Please ship me one copy of Atlantic Book checked below:

Hannon's Field Guide for Bass Fishing .... $ 9.95

Creatures & Chronicles from Cross Creek 9.95

Land that I Love (Hard bound) 15.50

Wild & Wonderful Santee-Cooper Country 9.95

Return to Cross Creek 9.95

Nature's Masterpiece at Homosassa 9.95

Hannon's Big Bass Magic 13.50

A Man Called Raleigh 9.95

Bird Hunters Handbook 11.50

Myrtle Beach Golf 12.95

Lures for Lunker Bass (Hard bound) 16.95

Best Bass Pros, Vol. 1 .... 10.95

Best Bass Pros, Vol. 2 .... 12.95

Deer & Fixings 11.00

Fish & Fixings 12.95

Hunting Hogs, Boar & Javelina 10.95

Trophy Stripers 12.95

Forty Years in the Everglades 9.95

Crappie Secrets 12.95

Virus of Fear (Hard bound—Ku Klux Klan Crusade) 19.95

Please cut on this line

Big Game... on a budget

Big Game... on a budget